CARTOGRAPHY *of* FAITH

DR. DIXIL LISBETH RODRIGUEZ

WestBow Press books may be ordered through booksellers or by contacting:

WestBow Press
A Division of Thomas Nelson & Zondervan
1663 Liberty Drive
Bloomington, IN 47403
www.westbowpress.com
844-714-3454

ISBN: 979-8-3850-1366-1 (sc)
ISBN: 979-8-3850-1367-8 (hc)
ISBN: 979-8-3850-1368-5 (e)

Library of Congress Control Number: 2023922831

Print information available on the last page.

WestBow Press rev. date: 01/10/2024

To my family. Thank you for providing a home built on amazing grace.

CONTENTS

Introduction

Personal stories are, in a sense, the fabric of life. Our personal histories and experiences take the shape of stories as we relate them to others. Life and stories are to be shared; in fact, they are shared whether we intend it or not because others observe our experiences. By doing so, they are at times part of our journeys and certainly part of our stories. When the stories are preserved in written form, our lives reach beyond the narrow confines of our physical presence in the context of friends and relatives to those unknown to us, inviting them to join us in the search for meaning, purpose, and mission in life. The communalities of human life make it possible for us to become active participants in one another's stories. This certainly sheds some light on the significance of the life of Jesus Christ that has reached us in the form of inspired and inspiring stories. In them, we find ourselves and are moved to be like Jesus Christ. In His life, we find meaning in our lives. Through his stories, we find a calling to share our experiences, to witness on His behalf the reshaping of our lives through His power. We can certainly do that in different ways, such as sermons and informal conversations. All of them are valid. Still, there is something innate in humanity that gravitates toward personal stories.

For most of my life, I collected stories of my learning, my interactions with others, and my observations within the scope of academia and chaplaincy. What moved me was a desire to engage lessons found in scripture into everyday life, to see the silent work of the Holy Spirit in my life as well as in the lives of others. It's a reflective journey, one worth engaging in and searching for in many random moments, I have found the divine engages us, builds bridges, and unites even strangers for a few moments. It may be that we only experience brief encounters. However, they shape significant meanings in our lives and yield experiences we yearn to share.

I have a confession: I selected these specific stories from my collection during a season of loss in my life. For years I have journaled, and the entries have always yielded material for publishing and sharing in speaking engagements and conferences. Yet these are the stories my mother enjoyed the most. She set them apart and participated in their revisions as they became speaking notes. In looking back and remembering the conversations we shared, these stories have yielded some fundamental constructs that unify them. I work under the premise that we are not irrelevant to God. We should search for the obvious work of the Spirit in our lives and in that of others. To see the obvious presence and activity of the Spirit in our interactions with each other requires from us a willingness to pause and listen. To stand still. That is a true challenge in a world that moves at a fast pace and where technology tends to deprive us of a meaningful direct and personal connection with others. Yet the promise of the Risen Savior remains: "Seek and you shall find" (Matthew 7:7 New King James Version, NKJV). These stories are a testimony that human beings are not abandoned by God; they provide evidence of the presence of God in human life. God is active in our individual lives through the Holy Spirit. Shared stories engage our Christian walk, which tells of our experiences, provide guidance in our journey, educate, support, and inspire.

First, the stories narrated here witness the value of the individual in the eyes of Jesus Christ. Each person is valuable to Him. He is constantly searching for them and calling them into fellowship through the silent and powerful work of the Spirit. Personal value is not fixed or measured by wealth, social status, or academic achievements, but by the basic fact that we are human beings created and redeemed by Jesus Christ. In these stories we find the poor, the rich, the healthy, the sick, the wise, the student, the child. And all of them are valuable to God.

Second, the stories demonstrate that human beings carry with them deep existential, and material needs. Absolute self-sufficiency is an illusion. We may not be fully aware of our needs or the needs of others around us. However, the Spirit touches us and brings us close in an attempt not only to identify a need but also to find mutual healing. Indeed, our shared stories are intersections, crossroads where God brings us together. In our daily encounters, we are called to fulfill the needs of others through prayer, greetings, presence, and so much more. The work of the Spirit on behalf of humans surfaces to reality through the most unexpected encounters.

Third, the stories we share demonstrate that isolation is not always good. It is important to resist the human tendency to blend in, disappear in the crowd, and live in isolated spaces. In our current states, we often welcome a level of isolation and call it privacy. Our stories demonstrate the need and at times the unavoidability of engaging another person at the crossroads of life. For such engagement with the individual to be possible we should be willing to say, "Here am I, send me" (Isaiah 6:7 NKJV).

Fourth, our stories are a way of looking back. A shared story is, in fact, a recall of what was. It is a visit back to the imprint left in our lives and on our characters at a specific time. We often can only move forward by looking back to the way God has led us and others in the past. We find courage knowing that in our good and bad experiences, God was always standing by us and strengthening us. We search for the obvious presence of God in human life in the past to experience it again in the present fragment of time. A fragment in time that is familiar to all of us. Looking back is a form of nostalgic life review, but it is also a strong, mighty reminder of conquered peace.

In looking back through shared stories, I reacquainted myself with friends, colleagues, peers, and strangers who gave me permission to share our stories, be that using a pseudonym or their names. I am honored for the trust allotted and grateful for the time spent in communion. It is my prayer that you will be inspired to search for the obvious presence of the Spirit among us and share your stories as well.

SEEING THE SPARROW FALL

"Did you find what you were looking for?"

I hear the voice coming from the distance. I don't have to turn around to know who is calling. Bill and Jason, lifelong friends I met four hours ago. I squint my eyes to look over the miles of open country, wind moving the tall, dry grass and leaves on the trees. I can see on the horizon where the grass touches the sky. The beautiful scenery unfolds with a soft breeze uncovering paths where others have walked. I wonder if they were looking for the same thing.

I hear the rusty door of Bill's pickup slam shut.

"Not yet!" I say, walking toward the trees.

"OK, we'll be here waiting for you."

That's reassuring.

He stands in front of my office door. I can barely recognize him.

"Ms. Rodriguez. I just wanted to say goodbye."

I look at the young man in front of me. Robert. Three years ago, he was a student in several of my writing courses. One day he came to my office with X-rays of his dog's stomach to prove that his homework (in a USB drive) had truly been swallowed by his dog. He asked me to call the veterinarian's office to confirm the story; all this to show me that he was not irresponsible. I remember meeting his mother, Elena, and siblings at an academic awards ceremony. Elena and I spoke for a while in Spanish, sharing bits and pieces of our cultures. She was so proud of Robert, her oldest son. I assured her he was an excellent student. She did not know which award he would receive. I knew he would be awarded the Academic Excellence Award and a scholarship. And now, here he is. A young man leaving for war.

I try to keep the conversation light. I ask him to show me how to properly salute, so I will know how to greet him when he returns. Work colleagues take the time to join the conversation in the hall. This is part of being an educator, I believe. You hope to teach something valuable, something that does not come from a textbook but from your heart; a valuable life lesson to carry into any part of the world. Something that would bring peace to the soul when the body is in the trenches.

We say our goodbyes, and I watch him walk away. I am not the only one who quickly wipes away a tear, painfully reminded that minefields are not simply found in faraway places.

> Dear Ms. Rodriguez,
> I hope you are doing OK. Can you believe it? It feels like I am all the way across the world. Never thought I would be part of a war, but here I am. I miss my family. I am doing well …

I have purchased an atlas. No computer-generated map will do. My eye catches the tiny print with the name of the town—a small line in a huge book, evidence of life somewhere outside the page. The road seems rather simple: Ardmore, Paul's Valley, look for the signs of Homer and Happyland, and finally, Calvin. I tie the passenger seat belt around the travel backpack containing the precious cargo for the trip. Friends offered to accompany me. However, this is a solo drive I promised Robert.

Empty spaces and small towns: These are what I see during the drive. The sun hides for a few seconds and the suddenly, rain. *This was not in the forecast!* Visibility is difficult. I pull over at a diner on the side of the road. It is a little pink house, but it says "DINER" in big yellow letters. I run inside, unsuccessfully avoiding the cold rain. A bell attached to the door announces my arrival. I see old-style booths, the kind without individual chairs. You get to sit close to the ones you love. It's emotionally warm in the diner. If these walls could talk, maybe they would speak of all that is pleasant in life.

> Dear Ms. Rodriguez,
> I got your care package today. Thank you. Thanks for checking on my mother. I write to her every day. I know she's worried. My last week at home, I made it a point to spend time with her. I have been thinking about that a lot. I think the toughest part is to reflect on everything I should have done to keep my mom and siblings happy all the time. That sounds all grown up. Maybe I am thinking about this because I am in such a "grown-up" place right now.

"What can I get you, dear?"

The waitress has no name tag. She gives me no time to answer.

"How about some chamomile tea? You need something to warm you up." She walks away humming. I don't know her, but she's looking after me. In the diner, everyone is talking and laughing.

"Here you go." The waitress walks me to a booth and sits next to me. *Why is she sitting next to me?*

"My husband is a farmer." She points to an older gentleman playing checkers with a young boy. "That's our first grandson, Jason; he's six. Jason's at the farm all the time, but he is going to college." She looks at Jason. I know that look. I see it in parents and friends when one of their loved ones wins an award or graduates. I can feel her hope and dreams for Jason spilling all over the table like slow-moving water, carefully stopping at the edges, creating a pool of hope.

"I've lived here all my life. I am Debbie. Where are you from?"

"I am from Texas, just a few hours away. I am visiting. I came to fulfill a promise to a friend and, in a way, pay my respects. The rain made it hard to see the road, so I pulled over."

"Oh! You're lost? Bill can help you!" She calls out for him.

Here they come. Bill and Jason. They sit, and it feels as if I am talking to family. I learn this was Debbie's mother's diner. Bill proposed to Debbie here. Last week they celebrated Jason's birthday here, filling the diner with balloons. This is a place of beautiful memories. Then Bill asks the most important question. "Where are you headed?"

> Dear Ms. Rodriguez,
> Time goes by faster over here. I was remembering the weekend before I left, when my mom took me to church, and there was this lady singing. I had heard this song before in Spanish, and it sounds different in English. The lyrics were talking about how God looks at this big world and notices sparrows. I remember seeing a lot of sparrow nests when I was growing up. It was a different time, I suppose. I wish I was a kid again. I just miss my mom. When I heard that song at church, there was nothing to say, just feel, and I held my mother's hands, and we both cried …

I have told Bill about Robert. I open my backpack and take out a bundled stack of letters and emails. At the top, I have placed the last letter, in which Robert has asked me to take pictures of his old town and the sparrows. Bill asks me why I have waited so long. I take out a Christian magazine to show him. It's a tribute issue for the Christian singer Del Delker, and the title reads, "I Know He Watches Me." I tell him that opening my mailbox and seeing the cover literally took my breath away and reminded me I had a promise to keep. As I talk, Bill simply nods. Something in his sunburned skin and wrinkled eyes tells me he knows how important it is that I keep that promise.

> Ms. Rodriguez, if you haven't seen a sparrow up close, let me tell you it's not a pretty bird. I started wondering. Why would God care? There are so many other beautiful birds out there! There is so much going on right now in this world; do you think He always counts sparrows to make sure they make it to their nests at night, every day? I think sparrows are something that only God would look after and check up on … something important, right? I understand that He would want to watch out for the little ones. That's what my colleagues and I do here, watch out for one another. I wonder if sparrows still fly out there in the open country where I grew up.

In my home, I sit holding a torn piece of paper with Elena's number. She asked me to help her two daughters with their college entrance essay exams. She thanked me many times. Her children would be the first generation of college students in their whole family.

I wish the phone could just dial itself. I wish there was a script for this conversation. Last week, I received the news that Robert would not return home. I plan to attend the memorial service. I am compelled to call Elena.

The phone rings once, twice, three times.

"Hola?" *It's her.* My heart breaks, wondering if she was just sitting by the phone, waiting for someone to call her and tell her Robert is still alive.

"Hola. Elena. This is Ms. Rodriguez."

Sobbing. She is sobbing. *She knows why I have called.* She mumbles something that becomes clearer as she takes breaths between her sobs. "*Mi hijo* … my son, Ms. Rodriguez … my son!"

The storm is still alive outside the diner. Meanwhile, Bill talks about his youth. He knows of war and loss. He remembers sitting next to his mother, radio on, random numbers being called out by the announcer. His mother always held a letter in her hands. One day after the numbers were read, she sat quietly next to the radio for the rest of the night. Even as a little boy, Bill knew one of the numbers read was bad news. His brother never came home. Robert never came home. Bill takes a deep breath, looks at the letters, and then at me. The longest conversation of the day takes place right there, in just one look. In those seconds we silently share words of sorrow, loss, and comfort. *You understand why I am here.*

"Jason, do you want to come with Grandpa to show this lady where the birds are?"

Are we headed out into the rain?

Bill watches me glance out the window and says, "Storm is passing. You'll have sunshine where you are headed. The ground is so thirsty you won't sink in the fields. Don't worry."

I believe him.

There is a plan. I will follow Bill to the crossroads, turn left, and drive five more miles. There will be a clearing, a space of land nobody will ever build on because Bill says everyone in the town knows that land "belongs to God." There I will find the birds.

Dear Ms. Rodriguez,

Today was tough. We get trained for "tough." Life trains us for "tough". It's late, and the stars are out. They look so clean in the sky, as if they haven't been

> tainted by all that's going on around us … Someone once told me that one day we will discover what we are really made of. Today I found out I am made up of faith and hope. Faith this war will end; hope that I will see my mother soon. I have a different respect for her now. It must have been difficult to raise all of us alone. We were all alone in our nest, with no father to help us. Today was tough.

I see the truck's blinker. This is my turn. Bill was right, no rain. I can see purple clouds in the middle of the sun. I am sure he's right about the dry ground as well. He works with the land every day, knows these details. My rearview mirror confirms there is no one in sight. I pull up past Bill and Jason, wave "thank you," and turn left.

> Ms. Rodriguez, when I was growing up as the oldest kid, I was the man of the house. We weren't rich, but we had food and shelter. I took care of my brothers and sisters. We would ride our bikes home as the sun was setting. Birds would fly all around us. I always wondered if they flew around looking for answers because they were curious. I remember wishing I could fly. I would be the one sparrow to climb out of the nest at night and try to make it to the stars. Fly without fear of falling …

Elena wipes away a tear as she tells me how much she prayed for her son. At night she would wake up and get down on her knees to pray for her son. She says she knows God was watching over him:

"God was the only one who could see him, watch him for me from so far away," she says. Then she asks me if I believe she will see her son again. She begins to sob. "Yes, I believe you will see him again. He lived his life with hope and faith, virtues God graciously gives us to share and comfort one another with."

Then I hold her until the memorial service begins.

"Grandpa, look!"

I turn to see what Jason is talking about. There they are! Out of the grass, out of nowhere! There are so many birds! Are they all sparrows? They gather and display a synchronized flight, separating into smaller groups and hiding in the trees. It's beautiful! They are singing, and chirping, and I can almost hear their wings against the wind. *Did He really see them all? Did He teach them how to get home? Did He give them the instinct to fly together, to care for one another? Does He provide the breeze for them at the same time every day to remind them it's time to return home? Did He give them the rain so they could feed through the grass, find food for themselves and for any baby birds in the nests?*

Back at the diner, I sit with Bill and listen to Jason tell the "bird story" to Debbie. It sounds so full of grace when an innocent child narrates it. I smile at the way he demonstrates the birds' flight patterns and tries to mimic their song. My soul longs to stay in the warm environment, but the sun seems to be falling asleep on the horizon, and I have a long journey home.

My car is packed with food, fresh produce, and kind thoughts. I get a big hug from Debbie, and Jason promised to watch the birds for me. Bill shakes my hand and tells me it was an honor to be part of this meaningful journey with me. He says that God took care of his brother and Robert. He reminds me that God doesn't lose track of any of us. We are always in His sight and in His heart. Just like the sun, this moment is slowly sinking into the horizon. I really thought I was going to get through this without crying. Bill hugs me as I sob a little. I have stirred painful memories in him that the sparrows have hopefully softened for him as they have for me. I hope.

Dear Ms. Rodriguez,
I have a favor to ask. Remember the town I told you about with the sparrows? My brothers and sisters don't remember the place; they were too young. But I remember the dirt road where there was a lot of tall grass, and we always saw the sparrows flying home. Would you consider taking pictures of the place and sending them to me? I have been working on a long letter for my mother, and I would like to include the picture. I have good memories of my childhood. I have good memories of her hopes for me and her incredible faith in God. It would be special to her. I would like to see the place again. I promise, once you get there, you will be surrounded by beautiful nature. You will be reminded of many of life's blessings. Out there, all the land belongs to God, I think it's the same here, even though we don't have birds … we all belong to Him. Faith and hope always, Ms. Rodriguez, always.

Regards,
Robert

Look at the birds of the air, for they neither sow nor reap nor gather into barns; yet your heavenly Father feeds them. Are you not of more value than they? (Matthew 6:25–27 NKJV)

GOD'S FLOWERS

THE AFTERMATH. WE CAN ALL RELATE TO THE AFTERMATH OF SOME event. What was the outcome? What happened in the end? More than likely, we can retell the event in the most detailed fashion. The difficult part is to move past it. It is more than a prayerful action; it is an action that often takes courage that God alone can provide.

Not all aftermath results are positive, and not all aftermath results happen right away. If we take the time to look a bit longer and listen a bit more, we can see that the Holy Spirit still traverses the aftermath and inspires us to be part of transformative journeys. The challenge is not to let any of an aftermath's outcomes go unnoticed.

I walk into the greenhouse with my friend Angie. She talks about the different flowers she has planted: bromeliads, Chinese hibiscus, chenille plants, lilies, and orchids. She tells me that these flowers are "OK," but her favorites are African violets. "They take more care, more time, and they are fragile," she says as her prosthetic hand touches the leaves of a pink African violet she has called "Hope." Hope. How perfect. I watch as she carefully walks through the aisles of flowers, touching the soil, touching the leaves. She cannot feel these with her prosthetic hand, still, she does it instinctively as every leaf has a different texture she can appreciate in her way.

As the sun filters through the greenhouse, I help Angie check the labels on each of the African violet pots set aside for our adventure today. These special flowers will soon be in a new home.

As I carefully attempt to park my car on the curb in front of my friend's home, there is apprehension in the unknown. I do not know what I will see. It has been thirteen months since I visited my friend Kathy. As I turn the engine off, it seems like an invitation for memories to flood my mind. *I remember.* I remember finding Kathy in the trauma bay at the hospital, her arm in a sling, bruises on her face, a deep cut on her forehead, sitting alone mumbling a prayer. I remember her tears as she told me her fourteen-year-old daughter, Angie, was in critical condition. I remember sobs as Kathy told me of the drunk driver who almost killed them. I remember her audible despair and sobs as she explained her daughter was in emergency surgery because they were trying to save her arm after it was crushed by the impact. I remember the surgeon's apologetic face, and Kathy crumbling to the floor, crying out the enormous pain she felt, the fear that was holding her. I remember visiting Angie in the ICU. She was pale, in pain, drowsy. In a gentle whisper, all she asked me was, "Why?" I had no answer.

A knock on my car window breaks me away from the past and returns me to the present. Angie. She smiles, and for a moment, her resilience and smiling face make me forget she has ever suffered pain in life.

"Come on!" she says. "I want to show you my greenhouse! Dad built it, but I am in charge of the plants." I see Kathy at the door, smiling and waving.

A greenhouse? It appears much has grown in this home in the last year.

Kathy and I sit at the kitchen table, watching Angie and her father load two small crates of African violets into a minivan. As we watch,

Kathy tells me that after the accident, when Angie came home, Kathy sat in this very chair, at this very table, and for the first time in her life, she was speechless. Kathy sat there all day holding the same glass of water. When words finally found her, her prayer was simple: "Dear God, she is Your daughter. Help us get through this. Use me to help her through this pain. I don't know what to do, but You do. Show me. Show us how to move forward."

I look outside at Angie. She's laughing with her father and joking about the "flower power" in the minivan. *It is as if nothing has changed.* She calls out to us. It's time to go. It's time to deliver flowers.

I ring the doorbell. Angie stands next to me holding Hope. I have been invited to participate in an activity that is now part of Angie's daily life: delivering flowers to homebound amputees. I hear footsteps coming to the door. Angie greets the lady at the door and then makes herself at home, running upstairs and leaving me to make the introductions. She knows this family. "Shelly?" Angie calls as we turn the corner and enter a room. I follow her.

The room is decorated in pale yellow with sunflower wallpaper and bedspread to match. It's a child's room! It's a little girl's room! Sitting on the bed is Angie's friend, Shelly. I notice the crutches next to her, and my heart breaks as I see Shelly's bandages; her right leg is amputated above the knee. *She is so young! She is too young! What happened here?* Angie hugs Shelly and shares the gift: Hope. I smile as I hear Shelly's joyous laughter. She is happy. Despite it all, she is happy. I watch and listen as Angie talks with Shelly. *This is more than a flower delivery.* Angie explains how to care for the African violet, and I watch as she encourages Shelly to gently touch Hope's leaves. For a moment, Shelly carefully touches the leaves and smiles. I hear Angie talking to her in a soft voice: "I named it Hope. I want you to take care of Hope and nurture Hope because you need to have hope this week. OK? It's going to be hard to not want to give up, but you gotta try. OK?" Shelly looks at Angie and nods. And just like that, laughter ensues again.

I stand at the doorway in awe, amazed at all that God has done, beginning with the healing of Angie to the receptive heart of Shelly to the creation of a flower. I welcome the peace of the Holy Spirit into the space, knowing God is watching.

As we drive to the next home for the next delivery, Angie tells me she has decided to train as a physical therapist. She sounds more confident and at peace. It's a fitting choice of profession. She looks pensive for a moment. "I know I am still in high school, but I am taking dual-credit courses, so I will have an advantage going into college," Angie states as she lines up the remaining flowers. "I just hope it won't cut into my time of delivering God's flowers."

I listen to this young woman as she prioritizes her life in a way she may not have done so a year ago. Thinking about and connecting with people she would never have met had she not spent so many months in the hospital. *Delivering* God's flowers? What a divine calling.

He has made everything beautiful in its time. (Ecclesiastes 3:11 NKJV)

NOT DONE BUT DUE

WHILE WORKING ON MY TERMINAL DEGREE, I STUDIED WITH A brilliant rhetorician. Well-known in the academic community for many philosophical contributions, he was a gracious, kind professor. Every day I walked out of class, I felt inspired—even after a significant amount of reading was assigned. Every time an essay deadline arrived, my professor would personally collect the documents from each student (no handing essays forward), always looking at them with great care and treating them as documents of literary genius. As some students scrambled for a stapler or appeared seemingly anxious at submitting the essay, he calmly and simply stated, "Ladies and gentlemen, it may not be done, but it is due."

I never asked if he coined the phrase. It has stayed with me for years and continues to be a mantra I live by. My professor never could have imagined the extreme teaching contexts where that phrase would serve my students well, or how it informed my presence in the classroom. There is wisdom in that phrase. There is caution to it.

The phrase and its sentiment have found their way to professional achievements as well. In my academic journey, there are celebrations for professional achievements. For example, awards for a professor's work by teaching peers and students. I have been blessed to receive a few. When awards are presented, I have learned to pause. I stand in gratitude only to see hubris a few steps away. I am reminded of that wise phrase, "It's not done, but it's due." It is an acknowledgment that the award at hand is for the delivery of what remains a constant work in progress—the labor, the achievement, me. I often wonder how to transfer this sentiment to my service to God and the necessary acknowledgment that God has provided spiritual gifts for *His* service, not for my personal accolades.

I check my watch: 7:20 a.m. Today, my graduate classes have a guest speaker, Dr. Evans. Evans is a collaborator in various projects cataloging the visual displacement of monuments. He catalogs architecture in visual modals. International organizations are slowly building around monuments in familiar places such as Greece, Rome, France, and Australia. Modern buildings are burying timeless monuments and their stories. Dr. Evans's research is quite fascinating, and I look forward to his presentation.

When Dr. Evans arrives, we discuss his work. Even though I have researched and read his work, I knew little about the person behind it. I find he is a very charismatic individual, very grounded and passionate about the research he lives with. As students arrive, Evans pats his coat pockets, searching for something. "I always wonder what I forgot before a presentation," he says. "It's never perfect, right? Still, time dictates delivery. You know, once I was at a symposium at your alma mater, Dr. Rodriguez, and I heard a professor say, 'It's not done, but it's due.' I have applied the concept reflectively to aspects of life."

How interesting! Me too.

That afternoon, on my long drive home, I think about how our words ripple through many lives and wonder: *Where is my professor now? Does he know how many lives became a bit more reflective because of a phrase he shared with us? Have I said anything profound that has affected someone else's life in a good or bad manner? How would I know?*

Maybe the phrase is a philosophical construct, handing over the imperfect, the potentially "less than" product when we know there's room for improvement. Maybe it's an invitational reminder of human kindness toward others in the collaborative actions to come: "What you have prepared is good. Together we can make it better." Maybe it's just practical advice: "Time has run out, the deadline is here, submit what you have." Language is power. Words have incredible persuasive sway and meaning on our beliefs, ethics, and actions. I think of my students and the readings they work through every semester. Text that sometimes challenges their cores and creates dissonance they must navigate and carefully examine along the way. If we explore meaning through a religious lens, revisit the powerful words, "It is finished,"[1] and expand on the complexities of what *began* once He spoke those words, what an amazing journey we would share!

My long day has come down to prayer and sleep. I crawl under covers as a word comes to mind: *accountability*. It is philosophical, invitational, practical, and spiritual. An opportunity for personal self-revision in mission and purpose. A way to preserve the growing dimensions of spiritual growth and the stories that are part of it. God calls me to be my best. We are called to be and do the best that we can in service to others as we follow the path of care and service to others left to us through countless biblical examples. We are accountable for every action that supports the process of self-revision toward a reverent, trusting heart and obedience to our Savior. I can search, but the reality is that I do not know what tomorrow will bring. "It's not done, but it's due." A start of the obvious: acceptance? Incomplete, imperfect as my work may be, God accepts it. Still, accountability lingers, and this humbles my life and brings me to my knees in prayer. At the end of any day, what have we done that was due?

Now devote your heart and soul to seeking the Lord your God. (1 Chronicles 22:19 NKJV)

---

[1] John 19:30 (New Revised Standard Version).

"HERE AM I"

As I lay on the hard floor covered by the blue blankets. *This is so painful. This is no way to sleep. How can anyone sleep like this?* I close my eyes, trying to visualize a starry night and clouds, but I begin to cry. *God, please keep them safe and warm.*

Not invited, I simply showed up.

Ten miles from my hotel somewhere in Rwanda, there is rumored to be a private orphanage. Visiting the country on a teaching assignment, I have booked several days of personal time. I must visit this orphanage. I don't know why. The director, Liliana, spots me coming up the walk. She is happy to tell me about the orphanage. The orphanage was built by a missionary couple who had no children. For generations, the family has maintained the orphanage. People from the family's church come and help them keep up the structure of the building, including safety measures surrounding the small space because it needs maintenance. I am sure there will always be a need for more.

After introductions, Liliana is gracious to give me the tour. Only fifty children reside here. Bunk beds with plastic mattresses and pillows line the walls. I see no blankets. As she walks me through rooms, Liliana explains that adoptions are frequent. Children here are healthy and safe. They attend class every day. They are not allowed to go anywhere without supervision. This space is their home, and the children know they will be safe there.

In the echo of polished concrete floors and wooden roof, I suddenly hear children laughing. It's recess. Liliana invites me to join her in the playground. In the playground, I meet Miko and Buma, two five-year-old twin brothers. They invite me to play kickball and quickly realize I am simply not a good athlete to have on their team. After recess, Miko and Buma return to their classroom, which has long wooden tables, small chairs, and a chalkboard. They hug me, and I feel both a sense of sorrow and joy in my heart. In these walls, in this space, there is laughter, there is joy, there is need.

As Liliana prepares a glass of boiled water and powdered juice mix for us, she tells me she was adopted by a Christian family at age four. "My family introduced me to Jesus," she says. "It has made a difference in the world. As a child, I could not fully comprehend how much Jesus was a part of my life. Now, as an adult, I cannot imagine a day without Him next to me. These children could grow up never knowing about Jesus. I may be the director, but my *real* job is to teach them about Jesus. And for those who are adopted, I pray that after they leave, they will remember the lessons shared here." I ask her how she knew this was the place for her to help and serve others. She smiles and says the story is too unbelievable. But I am familiar with those types of beautiful stories. They demonstrate divine guidance in our lives.

I look at my tin cup with orange-flavored water and silently pray, *God, what can I do here? What do they need?* My gaze falls on the outdoor area behind the kitchen, where pillows are stacked for washing. *Blankets!* Liliana explains how blankets must be washed daily to avoid insects and dirt, and to keep them clean. She points to a line of blue blankets under the pillows and says, "Those are the type of blankets the children really need—thermal and with the ideal fabric for the environment. The orphanage only needs twenty more for all the children to have their own."

Blankets. I touch the fabric and discover it is similar to plastic. I take a second look at the very thin "mattress"; it is plastic as well. *The ideal fabric for the environment.* There is something that can be done.

Two hours later, with the help of a translator and one taxi ride back, Liliana helps me unload twenty-six blue blankets and fifty new mattresses for the children. Those were all the blankets found in the town. Later, around the dinner table, I witness a child's faith as Miko's small voice prays, "Thank You, Jesus, for blankets and blankets, more than we need to keep us warm outside as You keep us warm inside." How self-aware have these children become?

It is time for me to head back to my hotel. The children are asleep. As we quietly walk past the rooms, I notice Miko and Buma, wrapped in their new blue blankets, sleeping on the floor. I wonder, *Why? Why are they sleeping on the floor? The bedding has been replaced! Mattress and blankets!* Then I hear the story. Tomorrow morning, two more children will arrive at the orphanage. Buma has convinced Miko that the new arrivals may be used to sleeping in beds, so they have given up their beds, just in case. I look around and see other empty beds and realize what is abundant in the room: selflessness. How long was my journey to see selflessness in action?

Hours later, I hug Liliana goodbye. It feels like I have been here for a long time, when in reality it has been but two days. With tears in her eyes, she says, "Isaiah 6:8. When I graduated, I got on my knees, put the diploma on the floor, and recited Isaiah 6:8. That's part of the story of how I ended up here." I look at the young lady standing before me, with such a big heart and such a big responsibility. *You did well by anchoring your gifts and talents to the service of God. You are blessed.*

That evening, back in the hotel, I notice the blankets in the room are just like the ones in the orphanage. How difficult would it be to sleep on the floor? To give up my bed for another? To be so grateful for something such as a blanket? I take the blanket off the bed, wrap it around me, lay on the same polished cement floor, and pray, "Here am I. Send me."

I heard the voice of the Lord, saying: "Whom shall I send, And who will go for Us? Then I said, 'Here am I! Send me.'" (Isaiah 6:8 NKJV)

THE BOOKMARK

Several years ago, I was gifted a bookmark. The bookmark is square, made of thick metal, and has beautiful Celtic designs carved on it. It is engraved, "Live, Laugh, Love." It is not a bookmark I would have selected for myself. It is heavy and slips out of books quite easily, which renders its primary purpose rather useless. Yet it is beautiful and oddly profound: "Live, Laugh, Love." An invitational phrase for the person who holds it, a checklist of sorts. *Which one have I done today?* Maybe the trifecta of pathos is a simple reminder of what to keep in mind over the long term. What to remember. It makes me wonder: *Could we sum up transformative moments of our lives into just three words?*

The week is dedicated to academic professional development meetings. For four days, professors from across the state will spend six hours in workshops, training, and lectures. Four days of learning new state policies in academia, listening to presentations from peers, and participating in faculty association events. Four days of driving to a convention center that seats three thousand people but has only five hundred parking spaces. I shake my head as I continue to drive, turning row by row, looking for an empty parking space. Finally, a vacant spot appears. It is so far from the entrance that I give up all hope of being on time.

I stand at the entrance of the main hall, listening to the speaker. I am late to the first faculty lecture series, and I quickly search for a seat. I quietly tiptoe toward the last aisle in the auditorium, where there is an empty chair next to my friend Dr. Michaels, composer and music professor at the university. I whisper "Hello," sit down, and to my horror, I hear the heavy sound of my Celtic bookmark fall to the floor, hit the tile, and oscillate in vibration. As heads turn my way, I look ahead, listening, entertained, as if unaware of the "situation" happening around me. As the bookmark becomes silent in its movement, my colleague whispers, "Your bookmark is set to A minor." I smile and try to control a small burst of laughter.

During our first break between lectures, Dr. Michaels examines the bookmark. He finds the metal to be resilient yet problematic as he notices its weight will never "hold still" between pages. "It is a rather persistent bookmark," he says. "Consider that every time it escapes the pages of a book, it will fall and remind you of three rather important general tasks: live, laugh, love. Don't you think everyone must have their own, personal, descriptive words to encapsulate a part of their life journey so far? An event worth remembering often?" I think about it and disagree, stating that maybe everyone *could* have such a thing, but it isn't a requirement that we *must* have these things. How many people do I know have an unexamined life? How many have examined their lives and made changes or improvements?

As we share our thoughts, I am reminded of why I enjoy spending time with my colleague, Dr. Michaels. We often share time over lunch at the university cafeteria, exchanging stories about student questions, assignments, theories, religion, and life experiences.

Still holding the bookmark, Dr. Michael shares that as a young disabled boy, he grew up at a time when few resources could help him succeed in school. There was limited medical assistance and no technology that could help him bridge that gap into a mainstream academic experience. He never spoke in class, so he was often forgotten or bullied. Music helped him to communicate and survive.

When his grandmother took him to church, he would listen to the choir, hear the harmonies meant for heaven, and say, "I want to write something for God." As a little boy, he prayed for the gift of music and dedicated its outcome to God: "Help me learn to play and write music for You and I will spend my life teaching others how to praise You."

I listen, reflecting on the many concerts I have attended where I have seen him conduct original creations of music performed by the university orchestra. Amid many standing ovations, he always looks up, points to the heavens first, and then humbly asks the orchestra to stand and accept *their* standing ovation. Such an accomplished individual and yet very self-aware of where his musical talent comes from. I never understood the blessing behind the talent, the answered prayers in every note he writes today. His story makes me appreciate so many things I had not even thought of.

"There you have a bookmark in the pages of my life's story." He smiles, hands me the bookmark, and adjusts his glasses. "My three words would be: pray, listen, praise. I challenge you to find your three in your story, Professor." He smiles and slowly walks away, using his support cane to probe through a busy crowd he cannot fully see, carefully touching the back of the chairs, and silently counting them until he returns to his seat.

Somehow, his three words stay with me as part of a "minister forwards" reminder. I follow him to our seats, with my advantage of sight and the challenge to engage other senses as he has done all his life. Pray, listen, praise: Those are the roots that sprout life, laughter, and love.

I will bless the Lord at all times; His praise shall continually be in my mouth. (Psalm 34:1 NKJV)

MISSING PIECES

I RING THE DOORBELL AND LISTEN TO THE RECOGNIZABLE SOUNDS of laughter and someone rushing to the door. There's something special about being a welcome guest. Then again, maybe it's because my eight-year-old friend, Chad, knows I come bearing gifts. Three days ago, my friend Linda asked me to babysit her son, Chad, on Sunday. "It would be for the *entire day!*" The exaggerated tone indicating the length of time made me wonder if this was a babysitting endurance test. Yet here I am with a new hundred-piece puzzle titled "Boats on the Harbor" for Chad.

As we begin working on the puzzle, I hear about Chad's school and friends. Throughout the day, we take breaks to read and take a walk. However, Chad is determined to finish the puzzle.

Late in the afternoon, the puzzle is almost complete. Well, as complete as it *can* be. Standing over the puzzle, we notice four pieces are missing. All our hard work seems like a sad waste of time because there are pieces missing from this puzzle box. Where in the world are these four pieces? By now, my joy and amusement for "Boats on the Harbor" have passed. I consider simply buying the puzzle again to find the four pieces and complete one of the "Boats on the Harbor" selections. Chad insists the pieces must be close by. After all, "Why would anything have missing pieces?"

Twenty minutes later, looking under the table, living room furniture, and bookshelves, I question my decision to participate in this search. I am about to suggest we put the puzzle back in the box when Chad shares an idea: "What if we *make* the missing pieces? We have cardboard and paint!" He shrugs, "Why not?" I consider the necessary tools: scissors, cardboard, messy paint. I sigh. I don't think babysitting should include such things.

In minimal time, we settle on a working area where paint will not create permanent damage to flooring or furniture. As I begin the tedious process of outlining pieces, Chad shares observations about the unique features of a puzzle. He describes it as an "everything story," where pieces come together to create one finished picture, photo, or person. But there must be some shared work. I wonder, *How do you know all this? You are only eight!* Yet his words begin to resonate. Here I am, carefully recreating the shape of missing pieces, cutting, and preparing them for Chad to paint, all the while knowing we will never have a perfect puzzle. There are missing pieces, and we are not good artists!

My part of the project is finished, and I watch Chad paint blank pieces into rather seamless transitions through the picture. He lets me paint the last piece: the blue sky. Once done, Chad looks at the puzzle and runs his hands over it. He says, "It's beautiful," and thanks me for working with him to finish the puzzle.

Overall, a pretty good babysitting experience.

At home, I pack materials for my Monday morning teaching. I accidentally kick my purse, which is resting by the door, and all its contents spill out. I see it hiding underneath the wallet, a napkin with four puzzle pieces. Scribbled on the napkin, "Found them! Didn't need them.—Chad."

I place the pieces on the table. On their own, there's no semblance of "Boats on the Harbor." The pieces must come together for a picture to surface. I remember Chad's musings on puzzles. The realization strikes: In daily life, we all need help finding missing pieces. Standing in the middle of our daily lives, looking ahead, uncertain of how the big picture will turn out, we often believe—in error—that *we* can control it. What must that look like from heaven? Humanity and its individual pieces, the ones the Holy Spirit helps us find for ourselves and others, or with help from others to create something beautiful with inspiration and grace.

The next morning, headed to work, I instinctively grab one of the puzzle pieces and take it with me for the drive to work. Just a welcome guest to remind me of the pieces of many journeys ahead.

Let nothing be done through selfish ambition or conceit, but in lowliness of mind let each esteem others better than himself. (Philippians 2:3 NKJV)

AN ANGEL'S GIFT

I MUST ADMIT THERE IS SOMETHING BEAUTIFUL ABOUT THE THOUGHT of angels around us all day. A guardian angel, someone next to you always, participating in your care. In a long past read psalm, I remember the psalmist reminding God about the tears the psalmist has shed and how each one is accounted for, kept in a precious space in heaven. I wonder, *How would a guardian angel react to our tears? Where did I read that when there is great sadness in our lives, a part of the choir of heaven ceases to sing? If that is the case, some of my life events have kept the choir quite silent for a while.* Angels. The idea they roam about a hospital hall, an academic space, or a hospice gathering is comforting. I cannot say I am ever alone.

I sit by her bedside, watching her beautiful face as she whispers her "big secret" to me: "I have an angel." Her eyes open wide, expecting a reaction from me. "My angel brings me pajamas," she whispers and then leans her head back on the pillow and laughs. Her laughter is so genuine it is contagious. Her angel brings her pajamas?

Five months into oncology treatment, my six-year-old friend, Sara, has been relegated to bed rest at the hospital. Her little body is fighting the illness, and treatment shows great promise. Yet she is weak and needs rest. The long stays at the hospital are difficult.

She misses her dog, Benjie; a neighbor cares for him now. She misses the flowers her mother planted in the backyard, and she wants to play with her dolls. Sara's mother, Lindsey, lives between work and hospital. It's just the two of them. *I wonder how they make it. Everything Beverly earns goes toward hospital bills and medication.* Beverly has sold furniture and home items to make ends meet, but it seems like it's never enough.

I listen to Sara tell me more about her pajamas. There are some with ducks, dogs, and little sheep, and they can all be worn in the hospital (even when she has an IV) because the pajamas are perfect! Who is this angel? I ask Sara how she is so sure it's an angel, and she tells me how one day she was dozing off to sleep and *felt* the angel place the pajamas near her feet! She opened her eyes and could almost focus on the angel, but she was tired. But she remembers the angel was wearing white! She shrugs her little shoulders and opens her eyes in a wide fashion and says, "It's an angel!"

I am touched by the story, and while charting at the nurse's station with my dear friend and nurse Tiffaney, I ask her if she has heard of Sara's friend. She smiles and nods. "Everybody knows! She shares that story with everyone! She will take the pajamas out of her overnight bag and show you!" She laughs and I smile. I also notice how the nurse has managed to subtly avoid answering the question.

As I complete my chart notes and log off the computer, the distress code for the Oncology Unit puts everyone into urgent care crisis mode. I rush down the hall with the nurses and see the light blinking over a familiar room: *Sara's room.* I immediately spot Lindsey standing outside the door, watching the team that has come to help her daughter. I walk to her and simply hold her as she weeps. Those few seconds of first response are always longer than a day appears to be. I look into the room and watch Sara going through a seizure. We have all seen this before. She is so close to going back home. I can't help but feel my tears. *My God, stay present. Send Your Holy Spirit to infuse wisdom in the hands that care for Your child. We are so fragile.*

When the code ends, a nurse stays by Sara's bedside, monitoring her recovery. On the other side of the bed is Lindsey softly speaking to Sara. It feels like a sacred silence. As chaotic and sudden as the commotion began, it has now ended, and a sweet silence envelops us. It feels like everyone will be okay. For now. I take in the scene from a distance and decide I will stay with them through the night.

Three hours later, I arrive to check on everyone and find Sara asleep. Across from the bed, Lindsey sits in a recliner with a blanket and a pillow, sleeping as well. *Where is your angel, little one? Certainly, the heavens have sent many angels to care for you in a special way, especially tonight.* I quietly walk into the room, tuck in the blanket under Lindsey's feet at the chair and sit next to her on the small couch facing Sara's bed. Listening to the steady heart monitor, I too fall asleep.

It is 3:05 a.m. I blink quickly to ensure I am awake. There is the angel! I watch as the angel tucks the blankets around Sara's feet and gently lifts the little hands so that they will rest on top of a small bundle. Pink pajamas. Then the angel quietly walks toward Lindsey's recliner, takes out something from a white lab coat, and places it next to Lindsey. *I know this angel!* The angel stops, looks at me, and quietly motions for me to keep quiet. And then the angel leaves.

It feels like it has just been a minute, but hours later, I hear Sara's soft and cheerful voice talking to the nurse who has come to check vitals. "Look! The angel came by last night. It came last night!" I see Sara smile as she folds two pink matching robes into one drawer. Her innocent hands extend to give Lindsey a robe. It is a child-size robe, but her mother accepts it with a smile. As Lindsey reaches for her daughter, I hear the envelope lying on the chair drop to the floor. I take a moment and walk out of the room as Lindsey picks up the envelope. I return with two cups of coffee from the nurses' station and sit with Lindsey for a moment as Sara continues to go through her morning health checkup.

"I gave up on good people a long time ago," Lindsey whispers. "I did not know the Holy Spirit still inspired people to be kind, so kind, and generous. You know, I skipped my work shift last night because Sara had that seizure, and someone just left us enough money to make up for that." Her eyes well up with tears, and she turns from her daughter to wipe them away quickly. I don't know if the tears are because of the kindness shown, the thoughtfulness gifted, or the reality that Sara is struggling. Does it really matter? Is it all not taken care of today? Has God not lifted the sun on another day for this beautiful child?

The day ends with reflection and a new appreciation for silent stewardship, emotional service, and inspiration toward goodness as the task of the Holy Spirit every day. The divine inspiration to challenge us all to care after one another. How easy it is to pluck the string of kindness inside us and let it reverberate in actions toward others.

As I walk through the parking garage, I manage to squeeze into the elevator where my friend Tiffaney, Sara's angel, is heading to her car. Our shifts have ended at the same time. She looks at the floor and willingly shares, "One day, I heard her praying. Sara, praying for pajamas! She had some, but you know it gets cold in those rooms. It was like something stayed with me, nudged me to understand that was an earnest prayer from a little girl, and it dawned on me that I could help answer prayer! We've started a nurses' fund for our ward. We select one patient every two weeks and keep a donation envelope where anyone can contribute. You know, it's not big donations. Sometimes change from the lunch you want to donate. Sometimes a little more. I got a few people from my church and community involved. With medical bills, there is a need beyond need, you know?" I watch her look out the glass windows of the elevator as we go up to the parking structure. Tears in her eyes, she says, "That girl really liked today's pajamas, right? I picked those! I *knew* she would like them. I got kids, you know. They seem to like the same things, and then you give them something, and they get all hyper!" She looks at me, and we laugh together. We share a hug. Tiffany is one of my angels as well.

What creates the urge in any of us to help those around us? What if we cannot help? What if we simply do not know how? How does the Holy Spirit help us to listen and take that initial step to serve others? Where in this process is the guardian angel that reports the events to heaven? I pause and am grateful for the privilege of observing the miracles around me. What a privilege to be more aware, vigilant, and ready to participate in any service placed in front of us.

For He shall give His angels charge over you, to keep you in all your ways. (Psalm 91:11–12 NKJV)

PRECIOUS ITEM

I FORGOT TO PRAY.

At 7:30 a.m., my colleague and friend Martin stops by my office and places a box on the corner of my desk. It is a gift from his wife, Tracy. He explains that over the weekend, as they walked through the botanical gardens, they saw this item and thought of me. I barely have a chance to thank Martin as he quickly heads out to teach his first class of the day. A reminder that I need to get to my 8 a.m. class.

I look at the box, the heavy lid, and the thick green bow. *What exactly made them think of me?* I carefully lift the lid and see the delicate, beautiful gift: a bonsai tree embedded inside a beautiful clay pot. Engraved on the clay pot is the phrase, "Precious Item."

At the bottom of the box is a pamphlet. There it is, in bold print: **Five Simple Steps to Care for Precious Item: Water, Soil, Housing, Pruning, and Light.** As I quickly thumb over the "simple steps" (in a brochure made up of six pages in ten-point Arial Narrow font), I feel an urgency to return the bonsai to Martin and Tracy with a note that would convey the sentiment, "Thank you, but I don't think so. This is too complicated." Instead, I place the bonsai back in the box and begin my walk to the classroom.

As I walk through campus, I walk past students, colleagues, the janitor who sings every morning while she completes a final walk-through of the building, the gardener who calls everyone sir and ma'am, and a few strangers I cannot identify as visitors or staff. Entering the classroom, I realize I forgot to pray in my office. My day is dependent on constant prayer! I try to remain inconspicuous as I whisper a silent prayer in the classroom. It is more than a ritual, my morning campus prayer. Every morning, when I reach my office, I take a moment to pray for guidance and for strength to complete tasks I may not know have become that day. I have already had a morning devotional at home, but I still need the presence of the Holy Spirit in *this* environment. Working in a secular educational institution is a challenge. Daily, I recognize my witness and ministry are by example. This is not always easy. I am conscious I must walk these halls accompanied by heavenly grace.

I glance at my lecture notes and find I have inadvertently included the bonsai pamphlet in my lecture folder. I glance at the five simple steps for care: Water, soil, housing, pruning, and light. Any precious item would thrive with those components. Any precious item would grow and take beautiful shape with these components. Precious items like the students sitting here—like Martin, Tracy, and me. Suddenly, my mind is inundated with reminders of Bible verses that speak of these components as necessary: *living water, seed that fell in good soil, house built on rock, the vine and the branches, the light and the way.* All of these thoughts because of the bonsai plant? Something inside me makes me smile and ponder for a minute at the extraordinary ways God reminds me of the ministry I am called to bear witness.

Back in my office, I consult the pamphlet to find the best location for the bonsai in my home. *Maybe I should think about naming the bonsai tree.* As I work, Tracy stops for a visit. She arrives as I am placing the bonsai near the office window to soak in the light. I am grateful to have the opportunity to thank her for the gift in person. She shares a detail about herself that I did not know.

"I am a minister's daughter," says Tracy. "I know how impossible it can be to share one's faith in this environment. We don't have the luxury to speak openly about the most important gift that has shaped our lives: Jesus Christ's sacrifice for us. In secular colleges and universities, professors are often given a list of topics to avoid. When I read the bonsai steps for care I thought: *This is what I try to do in my Christian life.* The precious item we share with others is our example, our faith. I wanted you to know that I pray for you and your work. I see you. I see your example."

Her words give me courage, but they also place a weight on my shoulders that I know only prayer will take care of. It doesn't simply happen in one location, right? As Christians, it does not matter our profession or our common/uncommon spaces. We are all called to serve as examples to others and inspire each other to continue on a path, no matter how challenging it may be.

At the end of the day, the bonsai has acquired a proper name: Faith. A visual reminder of *why* I pray every day is not only good to have, it is easy to share with others: water, soil, housing, pruning, and light.

But you shall receive power when the Holy Spirit has come upon you; and you shall be witnesses to Me. (Acts 1:8 NKJV)

HOW ARE WE DOING?

Evaluations. Performance reviews. Assessments. Feedback. Quality assurance appears to be a topic of many conversations today. There is a genuine interest to know how "we" (insert noun) are "doing." It seems like a day does not go by when I am not asked to provide feedback, be it a link by email, a smartphone text with a link to a company's web page, product reviews, restaurant reviews, and so on.

A few weeks ago, I called my bank to report a stolen credit card. The gentleman on the line was very nice and walked me through the entire process of reporting the card, closing the card, and going through all the charges in the account to verify if they were purchases I had made. I felt very happy that I was a member of this bank! This representative took quite a while to assist me, and by the time the conversation was winding down, the new credit card was in the mail (overnight mail for my convenience), and all was well. After completing business, I thanked him, believing our conversation was over. The customer service representative asked, "Would you please stay on the line to complete a short survey for feedback on the service provided?" Suddenly, our pleasant conversation became a complex numerical transaction rating the experience from 1 to 5. Our dialogue, once assuring and welcoming, now appeared clinical at best. How was I to rate such an exchange? Maybe I could just hang up before the survey began? He had been so kind, but apparently, that was his job.

I noticed my feedback was important. Not just with the bank but with many other locations. Feedback requests are everywhere. Surveys arrive requesting evaluations by mail or online from my dentist, local grocery store, even my optometrist! Printed receipts have numerical codes listed next to toll-free phone numbers you may call to evaluate the service provided (and identify the person who assisted you), at a restaurant, store, or hospital. Feedback. It comes down to one simple yet cautionary question: "How *are* we doing?"

In a reward-based-transaction world, what happens with feedback provided? Does quality truly improve based on *my* observation? What if there were no changes, repercussions, or rewards to any feedback, and we all agreed a "job well done is truly its *own* reward"? What would be left to improve? What would be the measure of *our* improvement from feedback? What *are* the measures of our improvement from feedback about *us*? Not in our perspective job roles, but as people, as Christians, as human beings interacting with others?

A colleague recently requested a recommendation letter for her teaching portfolio. Teaching assessments for an academic portfolio are unique. Not only are you interviewed by members of the administration, you also present a lesson to peers. This last teaching component is quite necessary to assess teaching performance and objectives. In my academic circle, a teaching assessment is scheduled to update teaching portfolios every semester. For a fair assessment, the teaching topic is assigned to the instructor in advance. It is a necessary occurrence, particularly in tenure-track appointments. There is a need to evaluate the teaching quality within the specific scholarly craft. Ultimately, the audience is a mix of future colleagues and administrators who act in the role of students. I schedule the assessment and wait for the evaluations to appear.

A couple weeks later, I hear firsthand accounts of the presentation from my colleague. "Two of the audience members behaved as disruptive students," says my colleague as she commiserates about her presentation over dinner. "How is this a fair evaluation? Why did they have to pretend? I mean, student evaluations are already difficult. It's feedback in numbers and comments from strangers, really." She moves food around her plate in a contemplative manner. "The whole experience made me think of how I interact with students. Every day in the classroom I find myself to be consciously effective because someone is watching me, assessing. I am being nice because someone is observing me every day, behaving because you never know who is recording you on their cell phones! Still, the peer review was even scarier than having technology and dual-credit students sitting in front of me."

I smile but quickly realize the depth of what she has observed, that "something" about one's self requires editing due to evaluations, due to feedback by others. Being a "good person" has no significant gravitas without the proper numbers to back it up. Still, you cannot ethically request good feedback from anyone; the feedback itself is created to query our performances. There is an element of potential fear of outcomes when it comes to feedback. Any form of feedback affects more than just our professional esteem. We often fret over lingering thoughts of what others think or speak of us. Whose evaluations keep us up at night. Friends? Coworkers? Employers? Family? Whose evaluations are fair or unfair? Personal? Objective or subjective? Does one's current state of mind and life detours come into mind as people perform their evaluations? Do we change our performances because of this?

A few days later, I am still pondering the conversation about evaluations, feedback, and how they often highlight imperfections more than growing edges. It appears that evaluation methods limit the person. All of us have different abilities and spiritual gifts that transcend borders of evaluation. At the end of the day, as Christians, we are evaluated by no rubric but through our abilities to be living examples of the life and teachings of Jesus Christ. Having accepted

Him as my Savior, my defective self is replaced by perfection that is not mine but that motivates me to excel in my self-development and my desire to serve God. I am motivated to care for others and my reward is fulfilling a mission of service for God.

Yes, there are human limitations of feedback toward each other. There are days we all fumble through rough terrain. And there are days we seem to sail safely through adversity. When no one is watching, in our service toward others, how *are* we doing?

Let your light so shine before men, that they may see your good works and glorify your Father in heaven. (Matthew 5:16 NKJV)

STANDING OVATION

It was not a lengthy prayer, and my inconsolable heart could not stop the tears from falling. Waking up after surgery, no pain medication, holding onto my physician as he helped me stand, I could feel every torn muscle in my body, and I prayed, *God, I cannot do this alone. Help me. Don't let me fall.* The news was far from the best: ten weeks. Ten weeks to walk again, to run, to become comfortable with movement, although any pivot would remind me of the hardware of the total knee replacements, the surgical steel inside both my legs. Ten weeks, and physical therapy every seven days.

Monday through Friday I would train at a special rehabilitation location where I would spend several hours working with therapists. On weekends, I would have a therapist come to my home and assist with retraining my mind to trust my knees to climb stairs, bend, learn how to get up from the floor, work in a familiar environment, and complete everyday tasks such as walking to the mailbox (which required an incline). Ten weeks to train my core to stand straight and walk without assistance. Ten weeks to learn and then a lifetime to continue exercises at home to ensure proper handling of weight-bearing objects.

I traced the calendar on my smartphone to see how far ahead ten weeks would take me. I may have to cancel the hospital chaplain residency I prayed for and worked so hard to ensure. This is the last requirement for seminary, and the one item left for me to complete.

I have stepped away from academia to enter chaplaincy full time, and now I may not be able to walk. That night was an experience of unbearable physical and emotional pain, lying on the hospital bed, weeping, asking God, *How will we get through this? I am certain that You have called me to this chaplaincy service. Why is this happening?*

Every weekday afternoon you will find the Physical Therapy (PT) Center off Rosewood Street parking lot full. The unmarked building is easy to miss, but when found, the space only allocates state-of-the-art equipment, knowledgeable and compassionate staff, and patients with hearts full of hope. The service provided is extensive physical therapy. A daily routine that, for many, is the last attempt to return to familiar spaces such as school, work, or home. This small critical-care facility is very proactive about helping children and young people recover effectively and efficiently. I heard one of the therapists share, "There is often a small window where a patient can completely recover from extensive injuries that required surgery. Sometimes at the most painful moments, we get the best results. The body remembers. Muscles remember. It is difficult to have physical therapy every day."

The recovery space hosts familiar faces. Families know and support each other. The *real* members are the patients, working on recovery, every day. The recovery is not just for broken bones and prosthetics, but also rigorous exercises to help patients learn to speak, walk, and move again. I was not exactly a "child" or a "young person" but was somehow placed in the facility as a so-called fast-track patient. I soon discovered that just meant therapy every day. That seems like such a long ago, but it really isn't.

Today is not a routine visit. I am here to sign up for potluck duty! The quarterly Families Together in Rosewood Park is next week! Families gather at the park, picnic potluck is offered, and most important, children feature an original craft they created that highlights the therapy they work on.

As I open the door, I am reminded this is a place of great hope. *Maybe I will see Tedi, my seven-year-old friend.* Not too long ago, Tedi witnessed my failed attempts at balance on a half-balance yoga ball. He watched me carefully as I attempted to stretch my arms while balancing on one leg and failed, over and over again. The exercise mimicked the muscle pull of walking up stairs. My frustration was silently perceived by the tears running down my face. The next day, Tedi presented me with tension bands to use with the yoga ball and assured me it was "not cheating." He shared, "It is scary to think you can't do what they tell you, you should be able to do. This helped me. You won't need them after a while." The bands were child-size, so they would not work for me, but Tedi talked to my trainer. I watched this young child explain the bands and pointed my way. The kind therapist listened as if being taught by Tedi how to do the job. That day, even using the bands to keep from stumbling, I worked harder than I ever had on my recovery. *It worked.*

I visit with everyone, including Tedi's mom, Vicki. She homeschools Tedi and cares for daily appointments. James, Tedi's father, works three jobs to ensure treatments continue. I learn about Tedi's project for the park. He has built a small wooden boat and attached a small propeller motor. The goal: to walk a few steps unassisted and "driving" the boat from the shore down Rosewood Park Lake. This is a big step for Tedi, my friend for whom I pray every day.

The hospital's physical therapy lacks the warmth of the Rosewood Center. I see the path and obstacles I need to go through in order to move on. It's Friday, and my residency begins on Monday. I need medical clearance that states she can run to a code, she can lift thirty pounds, she can be on her feet all day. And we hope she doesn't trip and fall, but if she does, this chaplain can get up and keep going.

I walk around the perceived obstacles and then back to the starting point. I quietly say a prayer and tell the physical therapist, "We're ready." After ten weeks, I was able to run the gauntlet of recovery measures and am discharged. But it was a pyrrhic victory. My friend Tedi was there before and after my recovery. I feel I am leaving a wounded warrior on the battlefield. So, I sign up to volunteer at the center because nobody should endure this alone.

Families Together day arrives. As I organize food on the long picnic table, commotion interrupts. I look up. There he is: Tedi, holding a remote control, pointing at the little wooden boat that is moving down the river at a quicker pace than planned, and James running after him. I smile and continue my task, yet everyone around me is quiet and still. I look up again and this time I see it: Tedi is chasing the boat, without a wheelchair, walker, or crutches, yet he does not notice this! When the boat stops, he turns around and jumps with joy! Even from a distance, we can hear Tedi: "Dad! I stopped the boat!" He looks around at everyone watching him. "Wait, did I just *walk* here?" I watch James, several steps behind, crumble to his knees, sobbing. For a moment, grace is tangible around us. As James reaches for his son, a standing ovation ensues from all the families and bystanders.

There are moments when the torrent of human emotion encounters the peace of the divine. And for a moment, our blessings seem crystal clear, our purposes undeterred, our prayers and hopes heard and continuously replenished. We search for evidence of these moments. Yet are they not always present in a way, waiting for us, a gift from our heavenly Father?

Hours later, the sun has set, and we are all heading home. I quietly walk behind James, who holds a tired Tedi, resting his head on his father's shoulder.

"Everyone should get one," mumbles Tedi. "Standing ovation. It's nice. We all work hard. Everyone should get one." He yawns. "You think my angel stood up too? Maybe the angel was flying next to me." His voice gets softer, and he yawns again.

James tenderly pats his son's back. "I think your angel, all the angel friends, and God were the first on their feet, buddy. All of heaven is watching you. Not just today, buddy, not just today."

That night I drive home imagining how beautiful a celestial standing ovation must be for all of us. I find the thought makes me smile and brings tears to my eyes. I pray this moment never strays far from my memory. Standing ovation. Yeah, that's something to keep in prayer.

The Lord your God in your midst, The Mighty One, will save; He will rejoice over you with gladness, He will quiet you with His love, He will rejoice over you with singing. (Zephaniah 3:17 NKJV)

TO WHOM IT MAY CONCERN

THE SMALL STICKY NOTE WAS STUCK TO THE BOTTOM OF THE BOX. Its presence was immediately noted as I collected the card stock of prayer requests from the hospital chapel's prayer box:

To Whom It May Concern: Who are you? What do you do? What do you know about COVID? About people dying? Do *you* read my prayers? I am scared. Thank you.

A small piece of paper with seemingly enormous queries from a stranger asking for my identity, purpose, job description, theology, and objectives of my day. I lock the box and place the note in my pocket, out of sight for now. Yet in my mind, as I work through the new routine of care during a pandemic, I write a response.

> To Whom It May Concern:
> I am a hospital chaplain. I am not called a first responder, although I am part of the team that stands at the front lines of triage, greets the ambulance, is present during patient intake, traversing the same hall the EMTs run. I sit next to the agony of hurting humanity and the unexplained inside the hospital rooms. You can find me where clinical teams chart,

where patients are transported, and in conversations where "recovery" is a descriptor used to evaluate and treat the pain that weighs heavily on a gurney. I am among the first three people called when someone is in physical or emotional distress; the person called when life is in the balance, the hospital room is too quiet when fear of the moment or surroundings brings into clarity the hazy questions we all have in our life review: "Did I do it all? Did I get it right? What happens now? How will I know if this is it?" And a rather common question right now, "Is this truly God's will?" Sometimes the only thing patients need is a little grace, a reminder of divine mercy, a prayer to help them move past this present point in life. Whatever hope you bring to the hospital will be nurtured.

My work schedule is often determined by you. If something goes wrong in the middle of the night, I will show up. There will be an urgent page, and I will travel down the dark, lonely highway back to the hospital with its bright lights, a city all to its own. If I am already in the hospital, resting in an on-call room, I will find you. I will be your advocate, a voice among many that will encourage you, be honest with you, participate in your plan of care, sit with you until calm brings rest from pain. I will stay until you say what needs to be heard in the moment, until you share what is in your mind and heart, until your stories are completely told, or until your silence finally lets you rest again. I used to have a "set" schedule. Now I am just here most of the time. See, I care for patients and their families, but also for the staff—my colleagues.

Most days are spent nodding and waving at colleagues. The emotional space is crowded, but the hallways are vast and quickly emptied. Seldom is the day I do not walk quietly past someone, staring out the floor-to-ceiling windows in the lobby, captivated in thought, in emotions, watching and waiting for the world to turn from inside. Somedays I am fortunate to catch a friend boarding the same elevator (only two of us allowed at a time). There are so many conversations left hanging on our hospital halls—no frames, just bare unanswered questions, suspended as if we are coming back to them someday to "hang them up properly," not just leave a hole in the wall, in our hearts. For amid a conversation, we are called away, reminded that the daily is not about us. It never is. The daily is about others, service to others, always. For this ministry of healing I belong to is all about mission and service. Right now, that mission requires the crossing of a gauntlet as I have never seen, full of decisive, defining moments, both in crawling through the dark trenches or traversing the cloudy fields.

I have met COVID-19 up close. The introduction was brief, and then pieces of me had to adjust. Now I wear scrubs under all the PPE and recognize different color markers on the floors that lead to decontamination, emergency, and exit. A picture of me without the PPE is laminated and attached to my trauma badge, signed, so you will know who is under the mask, know my smile. I want you to realize that even though we are in a difficult moment right now, we are not alone. I believe we remember days of smiles, hugs, and camaraderie with our families, loved ones, and dear friends. So when I read prayer cards, truly there is no doubt that it is God's will that we *will* smile, sing, laugh, and hug again.

Your prayer requests are on my mind and on my lips all day long. Even when the faces of those whose names are signed on a prayer card elude me, there is something about the penmanship, the tear-stained lines, the drawings of a flower or a heart in mindful marginalia that makes my heart ache and reminds me of one fact that grounds me during the longest of days and nights: We are not irrelevant to God. The prayer of those before me: "I will not let You go unless You bless me" (Genesis 32:22 NKJV), is one God answers with strong, mighty, delicate care. I pray all day long. I stand aside during codes, praying, observing until the body can no longer sustain, and the limitations of human effort are recognized. When the blood is on the floor, physicians shake their heads and step aside for the chaplain, for prayer. I may be the one who delivers the last words of comfort, the final precious message to a beloved family, child, friend, so I must pray all day long. Prayer is a necessity; it is air to thirsty lungs.

Even with technology, COVID-19 has designated me a lonely survivor, often the last person your loved one will see. Amid despair, when loved ones cannot be together, I am allowed through the doors to see them. I coordinate tele-visits and do my best to ensure that if your loved one is inside the hospital, separated from you, he or she will see, hear, feel you close. I will hold the medium of communication, be that a smartphone a tablet, anything to connect families. I sit with the family in this way as a most intrusive yet welcome guest. I listen to words of encouragement, regret, love, and forgiveness. Words light with emotion, heavy with desire to be where I am at. Often, no matter history or dynamics, there is not one family member who would think twice of trading places with me at a moment of loss for the privilege of holding the hand of a loved one is priceless. I feel the loss, too, and will care for your loved one as he or she is transported out of the hospital.

There appears to be no shelter for our breaking hearts, no comfort for our bodies in the elements as we all engage in bereavement outdoors. At a distance from the hospital, I see families gather, waiting for news, waiting to know what happens next. Sun, rain, wind, and cold morning temperatures, the elements do not deter the necessity for comfort. From a distance, I talk to the family and ask about their loved ones. I hear stories about traditions kept and unexpected life moments. For a while, families will rejoice in the color those memories bring to their present monochromatic existences, a lackluster future that feels impossible without one who has died. Between these emotional wars, we laugh. But the "rest" has not happened yet. Eventually, someone's voice will crack, tearing the seamless ribbon of memories we have managed to carefully tug at, and we remember why we are together. Closure is a resting place that eludes us right now.

I bear no judgment for anyone. Instead, as I write, there is a conscious recognition this pandemic has forged a strong common denominator in relationships among strangers. Do you feel it? Hope. The Holy Spirit nurtures that in us. In prayers, every day there is a reminder of hope. It arrives as an unexpected gift: time. It moves us from one day to the next, offering opportunities to serve others, to be among love and forgiveness. Life is so fragile. I am scared too. My solace comes from scripture and prayer. I don't know if you have a Bible, but I included a small one with a list of my favorite psalms for you. I believe they will comfort you, and I pray they will bless you. I do

believe we are meant to be a blessing to each other.
Not just now but always.

In the silence, I place a small package containing a Bible, business card, and personal pager number in the chapel with only a prayer to guarantee "To Whom It May Concern" will pick it up. It was 2 a.m., a quiet time in the chapel. If you stand at the left corner of the room, the stained glass windows create a faint shadow of a cross visible through the "busy" carpet. Fourteen hours later, my day has ended. I am home, safe, on-call with three pagers on the table. As I cry my day out—narrating the losses, gains, and exhaustion to God—the familiar sound of my pager fills the quiet apartment. A text reads, "Thank U, chaplain. Prayers 4 U.—Psalm 23."

A PSALM AND A PRAYER

Standing next to the fountain at my university, I look around, trying to find her. I peek through students walking past me in a different direction. Some notice me and dodge me; others are too busy reading on their smartphones and accidentally nudge me with their backpacks. Yet at the right moment, the crowd of students getting inside the university spaces out enough to where I can see her. There she is! There she is! My daughter!

There are certain statements and questions to which all college professors can relate. They come from students, simple statements and questions such as, "Are we doing anything important in class today?" Or, "I didn't complete today's homework. Does that matter?" Also, "Do we have to read the essays you assigned us, or is that optional?" And rarely but sometimes, "I can't attend class because I have a court appearance regarding my anger management. Here's the note." The appropriate response for the last one is to take the note quickly and discreetly and politely say, "Thank you. I hope all goes well."

I think about this as I turn the corner into the university parking lot. It's early morning and another day of teaching. Sitting on the bench next to my office is my friend Monica, staring at the floor, tracing the patterns of the carpet with the tip of her shoe. It's 6:30 a.m. She looks up, smiles, and immediately invites me to sit with her and chat. Monica is part of the overnight custodial team at the university. On any day, if I get to the university early enough, I see her pushing a yellow trash can, cleaning bathrooms, vacuuming lengthy halls, and wiping windows. She always waves at me. Sometimes I am lucky enough to have her stop by for a visit. She talks about her family, and for a brief part of the day, I forget about grades, essay prompts, and class preparation. She is very kind.

This morning Monica has a request. Next week is Bring Your Daughter to Work Day. She says, "I don't want my daughter to see me being a custodian. I want her to be more than I am. I want to provide for her so she can do better than I did." Monica's request is simple: Would I be a mother for a day? Would I let her daughter walk with me, enter the classroom, and see what teaching is all about?

She explains that her daughter wants to be a teacher and tells me about all the books her daughter likes to read. I see the excitement on her face as she describes the science and math homework her daughter brings home. She cannot help her daughter with the assignments, but she makes sure the assignments are always done! As I listen, her schedule comes to mind. She works through the night. Time with her daughter must be so precious yet limited. I understand what she wants to provide, but my heart breaks just a little bit and think about what it would be like to be a role model for her eleven-year-old daughter. Still, I agree to have her daughter shadow me for a day. I remind her of the university's policies and what she needs to request from our department chair to get permission as well. She listens attentively and goes to the task right away.

I take a quick detour to my department chair's office and find her quietly preparing class, sipping a cup of tea. She listens to the request, and I ask her if this is something the department would allow. "Well, Dr. Rodriguez, you will need to sign a few forms and liability waivers, but I will certainly approve it. You know, this is quite an honor, what this lady is asking you to do. Do you realize that?" I nod. "I will get you a student supply pencil case and a nice notebook for her. We have nice backpacks too. Pick a few books of poetry or classics to include in there. You said she's how old?" I watch my department chair pick up the phone and call the campus bookstore. Interesting how I forget to notice the kindness around me. With much gratitude, I return to my office.

Over the weekend, I find that I am overpreparing for the course material I will teach on Bring Your Daughter to Work Day. I have prayed about it and contemplated how this experience will affect the young girl. *God, please let everything go well, and take care of us!*

The day arrives, and Monica introduces me to her daughter, Bianca, who is wearing a pink pleated skirt, a pink blouse, pink socks, and a pink ribbon in her hair. We sit for a moment, and I hand her the thoughtful backpack full of goodies from my department chair. The pencil box is shiny and has sharpened pencils of many colors, a colorful eraser, highlighters, pens, and a small notebook to take notes. Bianca looks at me, her eyes big in surprise, and asks if all of this is for her. Of course!

I tell her what my days are like, walk her through our office suite, introduce her to some teaching colleagues, and watch her enthusiasm as she picks up the pink backpack. We head for the first class. As we walk, I look back at Monica, who has entrusted me with her precious child. She smiles and nods. *Dear God, let this day go well, and walk with us every step.*

We arrive at the classroom ten minutes early. We sit on a bench outside the classroom as students walk by, and some go into the classroom. Meanwhile, I pull out a small book of psalms. I open the book to Psalm 31. Bianca asks if I will teach from that book. *No, this book is to teach me.* I tell her that before I walk into any classroom, I read a psalm and pray. It has become a necessary ritual for me. She looks pensive then asks, "You do this so angels will come to sit in the classroom?" How young and wise!

I give her a task. We have three classes to teach today, and she is now responsible for psalms and prayers before each class. She hesitates for a moment but then smiles and takes the book.

9:00 a.m., Rhetoric II. Bianca takes on her task: "In thee, O Lord do I put my trust. Psalm 32:1 NKJV." Then she prays, "Please help everyone be nice today."

10:45 a.m. Composition I. "For thou art my rock and my fortress, therefore for thy name's sake lead me, and guide me, Psalm 32:3 NKJV." My daughter prays, "Dear God, please let an angel sit next to me, and let another one stand next to the teacher."

1:15 p.m., World Literature. "The Lord is my Shepherd; I shall not want. Psalm 23:1 NKJV." Bianca's last prayer, "It's been a long day. Don't forget us! And don't let anyone fall asleep in the classroom."

The day passes, and by 4:00 p.m., Monica and Bianca are ready to head home. Bianca tells her mother about the book and the prayers. She carefully takes out the book of Psalms from her backpack and hands it to me. But I think that every teacher should have a book like that. I tell her this and gift the book. She looks at her mother before taking the book, and on approval, she smiles and takes the book, holding it ever so carefully.

Early morning, another day of teaching. I see a brown paper bag placed in front of my office door. Inside is a red apple and a ten-year-old girl's handwriting on a pink piece of paper: "I will read and pray for you today while I am in school so that angels will come to hear you teach and help you." I smile, knowing they are already there.

I will instruct you and teach you in the way you should go; I will guide you with My eye. (Psalm 32:8 NKJV)

BENT BUT NOT BROKEN

I WALK INTO THE HOSPICE OFFICE AND LOOK FOR MESSAGES. No emergent situations, just visits. I go through the routine of signing in. There it is. I almost did not see it. A note from the receptionist: "New patient. Moved in; asked for a visitor; end-of-life conversation. Just talk." *Just talk*. I have learned end-of-life conversations are anything but "just talk." These are often heavy conversations with difficult questions. Often the questions do not have an answer. *He just wants to talk*. His name is Calvin. He's a farmer who has moved from Nebraska to Texas, where his children reside. I glance at the birthday note. *Is this a mistake?* He is 101 years old. Calvin, what have you seen and lived through, my friend?

"Have you seen the corn when it's growing on the stalk?" Calvin asks. I shake my head no. "Well, there is always one little group, a section of the cornfield underestimated by everyone. Often ignored, but that is where the real growth is happening. The stalks get heavy with nothing to show for it at the beginning. They bend toward the ground. That's all they do: bend. They don't break. One day when picking the crop, you see that little forgotten section, the one you gave up on, and notice pristine corn. Beautiful. Maybe it's bending, moving nutrients to the right places. Who knows? But I see it and always stop the truck and think, *That's me.* My entire life, God has worked with me. I have been planted and replanted in good soil, and still forget to count my blessings. When life gets complicated, I walk the fields, and I find those stalks and remember that my God is true. And I thank Him for letting me toil in His creation. I am just a farmer who loves Him. But I have my struggles too. He will let me bend, but He won't let me break. That's the challenge: to realize He won't let us break. Bend into the wind, and let grace, forgiveness, and mercy visit with you. That's harder said than done."

He leans into the bed and closes his eyes. I imagine Calvin standing in the field, searching and surveying the bent stalks. He speaks in a whisper. "Why does God let us bend? If we are faithful, why do bad things happen to us? In your heart—in my own heart—I am sure everyone has wondered, 'Why do we have to bend?' Please don't tell me it's the nature of sin. At my age, I have seen a lot."

I sit in silence. I want to say something, but nothing of value has reached my lips. I, too, have been replanted and still search for meaning made clear in my life. I, too, long for the coveted answer to the large question in life: "Why?" Am I also the proverbial stalk, bending and waiting for mercy and grace? Or does it simply mean there is something good happening in my life, hence trials and tribulations have found my address? I clear my throat and decide to be honest: "I don't have an answer. I cannot speak to the struggle of others. I know what it's like to be on the verge of breaking. Sometimes the break seems inevitable. Living in fear when there are promises of hope and salvation at every turn I take. What I do know is that answers often come with prayer, talking to God as if He is sitting right next to me. When I feel the bend and recognize it in my life, I pause and look at what is surrounding me, where God has placed me. Sometimes that is difficult to understand. It is difficult to comprehend in our sense of time."

My life, compared to a cornstalk. How did we get here?

He opens his eyes and smiles at me through a tired body and a weathered spirit. "That's the most honest thing anyone has told me since I got here." We sit together for over an hour. He talks, we pray, I listen. As he falls asleep, I quietly exit the room. At 101 years of age, there is still both mystery and clarity in our life journeys.

That evening, I pray for Calvin. The Holy Spirit, present in our conversation, moved two people to reflect on the way we can see things but not really *see* them. Bent but not broken. It's a familiar adage, words I have heard before but not truly *felt* before. The metaphor can run on different paths, but the outcome is similar: self-awareness of how God works in our lives. Is it truly a mystery that we encounter challenges, joys, and the occasional soul replanting in our Christian lives? How many times do we look up from life-size mountains and ask why? I have lived through seasons when growing meant bending toward the wind, recognizing the need for divine intervention in the soil and the space around me. Strong winds will test any resolve, yet we can look back and see how and where God has replanted us for growth. The proof of this is the evidence of tailored care through every season of our lives. The substantiation is in promises found through prayer and meditation. For all of us who seek, there appears to be one most difficult task: to spend time in the complexity of growing in different ways into the call of service and ministry that God places in front of us. A season of growth. A sense of confidence that God may let you bend. But be confident; He will not let you break.

For as the heavens are high above the earth, so great is His mercy toward those who fear Him. (Psalm 103:11 NKJV)

FROM CHOICE TO PLAN

Choice. One of the most emotionally and philosophically charged words in our vernacular. When you engage in it, you are deciding and selecting between two or more possibilities. The very paraphrase of the definition demonstrates the complexity of choice. Still, as complex as the choice may be, we engage in it every day. Why? We all have plans and goals to achieve. And a plan requires choices.

We choose items by price, appearance, and name brand. We choose our friends by mutual interests and character types. We choose our homes by location, weather trends, and job availabilities. We labor over making choices for small and big plans. What choices weigh more heavily in our lives? Do we create a plan and deal with choices as they come? Do we spend time outlining the choices necessary and then watch the plan unfold?

As Christians, "choice and plan" have specific gravitas; there is a confluence that occurs. While choice may engage many facets of an exploratory excursion into free will, there is value in simply exploring choice as an overall character, architectonic approach in our daily interactions. How do we exercise wisdom in choices made? In moments of uncertainty, when we cannot fully see a plan developing ahead, how do we engage wisdom to move from choice to plan?

Of all the things Solomon could have, wisdom was his choice. Wisdom can engage other qualities, such as compassion, humility, empathy, love, a willing heart to serve, leadership, and purpose. Our choices are ongoing.

I think about this as I observe students going through academic advising during early registration at the university. Every semester, professors are encouraged to "work the registration tables" and serve as advisers for students asking questions about individual courses. Students register for courses on the spot. But first, most like to visit with professors and collect information to make an informed decision on how to continue (or begin) their academic pursuits. I sit next to my colleague, Dr. Sanders, who will retire at the end of this term. A brilliant professor, we often engage in discussions about ethics, language, and religion and somehow, we always manage to appreciate each other's opinions. Today, he speaks of retirement plans and lessons learned after forty-eight years of teaching. Forty-eight years of teaching! How many academic and social changes have you witnessed?

His reflections are interrupted by a young student standing in front of our advising table. "I have no clue," she says. "I chose philosophy because I need to find myself, find some purpose in my life. What do you recommend?"

The question is familiar, but I venture to say that many professors always tread lightly on this line. It is just one step from the abyss. Before I can hand her a course listing, Dr. Sanders reaches into his briefcase and pulls out a Bible.

"Here you go," he says, placing it in front of the student. "Begin here. Read every day. The 'self' is not able to engage in purpose without the sacred. Understand that, and other choices become easier."

The student glances at me, carefully, slowly picks up the Bible, mumbles a "Thank you," and exits the building. Dr. Sanders casually adjusts his tie as I sit still. We are both aware he has chosen to consciously break all potential proselytizing rules by university standards. Still, he is retiring in a few months, and I am confident he will still have his job tomorrow.

"I wish someone would have done that for me when I began," he says. "I hope my legacy includes a way to encourage students to search for answers in the *right* places and choose well." His voice shakes, and I see something different evolve. My friend, a professor, realizes *this act* was the best lecture given in forty-eight years.

The sacrifice made for our choices to exist outside the mundane into the sacred and holy is a precious gift from God through Christ. "For I know the plans I have for you … plans to prosper you and not to harm you … plans to give you hope and a future."[2] To embrace that promise is the way to surrender all and give way for wise choices toward God's plan for us.

> All Scripture is given by inspiration of God, and is profitable for doctrine, for reproof, for correction, for instruction in righteousness, that the man of God may be complete, thoroughly equipped for every good work. (2 Timothy 3:16–17 NKJV)

---

[2] Jeremiah 29:11 (NKJV).

TRUST THE PATH

It is rare to receive an emergency code page at 10 p.m. with no room number. At the hospital, I am directed to the cardiology unit. I stand at the doorway of the room. Lights are dim; a gentleman sits in the bed, reading a Bible. The patient's closet is open. Inside, a priest's outfit is neatly hung. Next to him is a container with ice water for drinking. No flowers in the room. *What am I missing? Where is the emergency?* The nurse tells me that earlier this week, the patient coded, but the teams were successful in "engaging his heart." Since then, the patient has been quiet. He filled out a DNR and has spent time crying, praying, and reading the Bible. His name is Peter.

I walk into the room, closing the sliding glass door a bit for privacy. I introduce myself. He offers me a seat in a chair next to him. Closing his Bible, he tells me he *finally* got to Proverbs. Finally got to Proverbs? I glance at the closet. Is he not a priest? He notices my gaze and answers what I have not asked. "Yes. As a priest, I could have read the Bible, but other books were placed in front of me, books of policy and traditional rituals. Well, you understand." He speaks softly. "Yes, I just got to Proverbs. I was so consumed with terms like *infinity* and *eternity.* I cannot remember how many times I told my parishioners, 'This is God's will,' 'Trust the path,' 'Things happen for a reason,' and, 'Your family member is in a better place.' But I had it wrong, didn't I?"

Peter tells me of his failing heart, a boulder of illness blocking his path forward. After much prayer, it doesn't seem the boulder will budge. He trusts God will provide a new path. He admits that getting to this path has not been without fear. Peter asks, "What would you do if God decided to leave a boulder in your path? Would you be disappointed? Do you question God? Do you use the time to commune with Him?"

As he speaks, his hands begin to tremble. I walk to the end of the room and collect a warm blanket for Peter. I need a moment. *God, how do I answer this question?* Before I can speak, Peter arrives at an obvious conclusion: "Paths are individual. If I trust God, I will wait on God, I will confess my sins rely on His love, His will be done. Still, I have a bit of fear. I am sure that is common."

I wrap the warm blanket around him silently, letting the moment run deep through our hearts and bones. The vacant moment where humanity questions the divine is always just a step away, but that chasm is quickly filled as the answers to our questions are truly all about prayer. I look at my new friend and sit next to him, next to his tears. I extend my hand as if offering the only human counsel I dare provide: "Pray. Earnestly. He is with you at this very moment. He is with us at every path." I sit, holding his hand, praying quietly, feeling the weight of the world in his palm, with the sudden jolt of realizing there is something much greater than us caring for us, always available to us, delivering for us.

The night finds us speaking about God and praying. While reading scripture aloud, Peter runs short of breath, and I am moved to simply read to him until he falls asleep. My thoughts and verse slip away to silence as the charge nurse enters the room and takes the patient's vitals. I look at her for a moment, and she shakes her head. This is the delicate nature of humanity. One day we read to others, and then one day we need someone to read to us.

Peter wakes for a moment as the nurse switches IV bags and hears me reading. "I have found peace," he says. "Please keep my Bible." He dozes off. As I continue reading, tears blur my vision. It appears the entirety of our space has paused for just this moment. No calls interrupt our prayers; no one else needs a chaplain tonight. How fragile we are. How mighty the hand that leans in for us.

Before the sun peeks through the night sky, an alert of a flatline is heard from the monitor in the room. Physicians arrive, and flatline runs its course. And then, silence. After forty-five minutes of verification and assessment of the patient, a prayer is requested by the attending physician before leaving the room. I stay, remembering the many boulders God moved out of my path, remembering how many boulders God has helped me walk past and climb over to reach a destination. I open Peter's Bible. Annotations and marginalia fill the corners of many pages. I skim through his notes and travel through the pages of psalms. I notice a fold in the corner for Psalm 23. What a familiar path, the one the Shepherd walks, ensuring no one is left behind. In the end, Peter's journey spoke of more than just trusting the path. It spoke about trusting God's path for us, the surrender of all that is borrowed. It's a familiar place to begin and continue searching for peace.

And the peace of God, which surpasses all understanding, will guard your hearts and minds through Christ Jesus. (Philippians 4:7 NKJV)

JUST TRYING TO GET HOME

It is one of *those* mornings when I am running late even before the morning alarm goes off. The to-do list sitting next to my car keys serves as a reminder of all that must happen today: errands, projects to complete, committee meetings, class plans, grading tasks, visits, and so on. Today it physically takes longer to get ready to meet the world than to complete any task. *How can I be exhausted already?*

As I pull out of the garage, I am greeted with heavy rain and wind. *I thought the meteorologist said it would just be cloudy.* At the streetlight toward my entrance into the highway, the wind blows a cardboard makeshift sign right past my car window. Running after the sign in soaked jeans, a light jacket, and a cowboy hat is a man. Fighting the wind, he holds on to the hat and grabs the sign. I watch as he returns to the corner of the intersection, where he lifts the sign to his chest: "Just Trying to Get Home."

The light turns green, and only a few cars manage to make it through the intersection, leaving me closer to him. I can read the sign now. Under the initial phrase is his plan: "Oklahoma Bound." He's headed somewhere and probably needs money. Slightly jolted into reality, I look around my vehicle. I have nothing to give him. I have my computer, an umbrella in the back seat, a bottle of orange juice, and my to-do list wedged between my purse and passenger seatbelt. My heart beats faster. I look at the traffic light. Red. The wind outside makes a howling sound that makes me look up, wondering, hoping the storm is not worse than it sounds. As I see the man standing in the rain, I am suddenly reminded of my morning prayer: "In all my tasks today, God, keep me focused on what is truly important." Well, here is the first task!

Keeping my eyes on the traffic light, I quickly go through my purse and grab my wallet. It's not much, but it's all I have. I open the window and immediately feel the rain and the wind. He must have been watching his surroundings carefully because he immediately runs toward my vehicle. "God bless you, ma'am. I am just trying to get home to Oklahoma, to my brother's place. God bless you."

He quickly moves away from my car, and as if on cue, the light turns green.

As I merge into the highway, I cannot get this stranger out of my mind. *What else am I supposed to do? There are so many like him. I may even encounter more homeless people on the next corner!* A feeling of great desperation takes over, as if I am suddenly responsible for him. I know this feeling. I focus on the rainy, wet road ahead and pray, "I don't know what to do, God. If you have a plan or a way for me to help him, please let me know."

God lets me know.

Just as I merge into the highway, my cell phone rings. The call is from my friend Debbie, a retired social worker, and Don, her husband of thirty years, a retired cop. Retirement did not suit them, and now they spend time managing nonprofit food banks in the area. Debbie is calling to thank me for volunteering with the food bank this past weekend and to offer me prayer for the day. They are waiting out the rain this morning and will soon head out to deliver some supplies to the food banks in Oklahoma.

Oklahoma?

The end of a long day finds me at a local diner, sitting across from Debbie and Don. Back from their trip, they took the stranger home to Oklahoma. His wife had recently died of cancer. He has a young son who currently lives with this man's brother on a ranch in Oklahoma. There were things to finish up in Texas and plans were made on how to come together as a family again. Once the man was laid off, there was no reason to stay in Texas. He lived in a local shelter for a week, working odd jobs and saving for a trip to Oklahoma to be with the only family he had left: his son and his brother. At the destination, Debbie and Don met the family and witnessed a heartbreaking reunion. Excited to see his brother, the stranger ran out of the truck into a familiar embrace and wept. A small child with a teddy bear ran out yelling, "Daddy!" He was scooped up in a big bear hug. *How long had it been?* Don tells me that as they watched the scene, he noticed the stranger had left the wet sign he had been carrying on the floor of Don's truck. He didn't need it anymore; he simply did not need it anymore.

"He told us that you were the only person who stopped for him," says Debbie. "He told us he didn't have anything but wanted to send his Bible to you, but I told him to keep it for a rainy day!" She laughs and wipes away a tear. This emotional journey has been long, and a tangible blessing has reminded us all of our ministry of service toward one another.

Debbie composes herself for a moment. "He was so grateful. I just told him, 'Listen, we are just all people. Happens we are all Christians here.'" She continues to wipe the tears away, but her voice cracks with emotion. "And we are all just trying, you know." she begins to sob.

I know. We are all just trying to get home.

The Lord will guide you continually and satisfy your soul in drought. (Isaiah 58:11 NKJV)

COUNTED BLESSINGS

I ALMOST THREW THE INVITATION AWAY. TRUTHFULLY, THE ENVELOPE (decorated with a blue, child-size handprint) had already made it to my junk-mail-shred pile of magazines, advertisement fliers, bills, and cards. On second inspection, the envelope had a familiar sender and a speaking invitation not to be ignored!

> You are invited to be a guest speaker during our Share Week at Heritage Elementary! We invite you to be one of the community and Christian volunteers who share an uplifting story about their work with our students! Our students are guest speakers too! They have a special program to share with you.

A second, third, and fourth inspection of the envelope makes me smile. The invitation is from Erica, a graduate school colleague who now teaches second grade at Heritage Elementary. When I call Erica to RSVP for the event, she gives me more direction for the event. "It would be great if you introduce yourself and what your profession, work, is all about. I am asking the speakers to share five positive reasons why they love their job." Sign me up!

Three weeks later, sipping lemonade from little green cups inside a small classroom with orange and yellow carpet, I find myself sitting on a tiny red chair looking at cloth totes filled with building blocks and bookshelves filled with big books! I have concluded that this event belongs in my top-ten favorite speaking engagements of my life, at least so far. When all guest speakers are done it is time for the next event. The second-grade students will present "Appreciation Monologues."

As the presentations begin, a pattern emerges. All the students must speak of three to five things they are grateful for. A young boy shares gratitude for receiving good news about the health of his hamster, for bike rides with his older sister, and for having a friend share a specific Crayola color to finish a drawing (after all, it was a color he did not own). Another student is grateful for her goldfish, the way her mother sings to her on the drive to school, and the new building blocks that she shares with everyone in the room. One by one, the eighteen students share what they are grateful for. The last presentation is from a young girl who has written a poem for the occasion, "Number Blessings." She is grateful for the blessing of sunshine and flowers in the backyard, for skipping and smiles, and for the quilt her grandmother made for her.

Every child shares something precious they are grateful for. Something ... *simple*? Or is it the fact that their gratitude is so honest and innocent? *Counted* blessings? Do they know they get more than just three to five?

At the end of the day, students thank the speakers by handing out individual cupcakes covered in red cellophane paper. On the drive home, with the cupcake safely strapped under the seat belt on the passenger side of my car, I begin to draft a list of things I am grateful for: a home, good friends, good health, job. Somehow, my list does not sound as happy, honest, and innocent. It's such a grown-up list! I don't have a pet, skipping ended years ago, and I am pretty sure my elliptical bike is not really considered a "joyful bike ride." My older, skeptical mind seems too logical about this list. After all, I have these blessings, but there is also hard work involved in nurturing all these things. What am I missing?

At home, I stare at the bright red cellophane paper covering the cupcake. I cannot remember the last time I ate a cupcake, just because. I smile. Someone thought of baking cupcakes for the speakers, and that is a generous gift that merits gratitude. As someone way past second grade, what could my day of gratitude sound like as that of a child of God? Have I begun to categorize blessings as "resolved problems" or "answered prayers"? Where do I begin to share the daily gifts of my heavenly Father, to truly engage in counted blessings?

The sounds of thunder and rain wake me up in the middle of the night. I lie in bed and consider a different form of gratitude, a different shape of counted blessings: phone calls from family reminding me of their daily love and prayers; Mondays at noon, when my work colleague and I walk to the fish pond in the middle of campus and feed the fish during our lunch break; the sound of rain that reminds me of second chances; the inspiration the Holy Spirit places in the hearts of my friends to send random emails to say hello; the sunrise I get to see every morning on my drive to work. For a while, I simply think about the unexpected brushstrokes from heaven that bring beautiful splashes of color into my day. The details that make me smile and remind me to walk a little slower to appreciate the moments I am gifted, such as the slow breeze that makes the dry leaves tumble in front of me when I walk by the lake, and the sound of a children's laughter that immediately makes me look their way to see what treasure they have discovered. Every detail of my day reminds me that God's presence and grace are with me in the moment. Maybe it's not about counting my blessings but recognizing there will always be blessings to count.

Every good gift and every perfect gift is from above, and comes down from the Father of lights, with whom there is no variation or shadow of turning. (James 1:17 NKJV)

THE ENDLESS REALITY OF FORGIVENESS

It is something we struggle to fully understand, I believe. Come, Holy Spirit, come. It is the intersections, the whirlwind of unexpected grace blowing through our lives, reminding us of something—a task, a conversation, laughter, prayer, forgiveness.

The elevator is taking a long time. I am in no hurry. I notice the cameras placed in every corner of the ceiling. My companion, the correctional officer, tells me people in this place appreciate chaplain visits. I believe the comment is meant to make me feel better, but it does not.

The elevator makes a creaking noise as if exhausted from years of service. I step outside to the hallway and notice the green tiles, just like the lobby: institutionalized. We walk through painted corridors, where the paint used appears to have been clean and pristine white at some time, but now there is no name for the color and shade. We arrive at yet another narrow door that, once opened, demonstrates only heavy, thick steel bars that deliver a frightening sound as locks are lifted. The officer holds the door open. I walk in and step aside as the door locks behind us. Three doors later, we arrive at a small room with a long wooden table, three folding chairs, and a mirror on the wall. *Is someone looking? Is someone listening?* The officer tells me he will remain behind the glass, "just in case." I nod as if it would make a difference for him to know I understood. The fact is, I am too busy counting the number of chairs and wondering, *Who else is coming?*

I think of the long drive here and then the quiet space in this building where forms are filled out to allow a visitor. I am here because ten years ago, this man was my college student, a great writer, full of promise, and he found a short story I had written and searched for me. I cannot remember the name of the short story, so I look around the room, conscious that someone is watching. He could have crafted his life in a beautiful way if he hadn't ...

The door opens, and a man in shackles enters the room. A lawyer, I assume, is with him. The feeling of space is real as if the table between us is a zoning line where conformity is necessary lest you fall off the edge of the table, forgotten. I watch as the man shuffles to one of the chairs, and the attorney sits next to him. There is a pause as I have taken the scene in, and I am now able to take the third chair and sit. It's as if time has a different speed in this room, a speed that takes me back ten years, where I barely recognize the face of this individual, and nothing around us speaks of prison life. He's not a student anymore; he's an inmate.

"The meeting was requested by the inmate," states the lawyer. "Nobody is listening to our conversation or 'religious absolving,' so we may proceed." *What is he talking about? I am here to listen, not to absolve.*

When the lawyer finishes the introductions, I look at my student. "Tell me why I am here."

For two hours, I listen to my former student speak of gruesome, proven truths. The files are open. He will move to a different location and appeal his sentence. His life changed in a moment, truly changed in just one moment. Now his life is dictated by others who control every second of his day. Even so, time here has proven useful in only one way: the Bible. He has joined a group of inmates that meets with a chaplain every week and talks about scripture, faith, and God. He tells me that growing up, he had many Bibles around him but never read one. Now, the Bible he has in his cell has been marked and re-marked, and he finds something new to talk to the chaplain about every time. He speaks as if we are somewhere else, having a casual cup of tea, sharing our day. But then the silence creeps in, and I realize I have only been listening, not engaging in the conversation.

"I can't believe you came," he tells me. I hear a crack in his voice. He is wrapped in blankets of shame, uncertainty, and judgment. He is low on hope. "I have a question, and I thought, well, you are a chaplain, and you knew me before all this, and well ... how many times can we be forgiven? Here, I have time to read, think, and reflect, and I wonder if people ever forget the past and start new, like strangers. *Really* forgive and forget. Even here."

Is this what you wrestle with in the night? Are you seeking an angel to hold on to before the sun comes up? Have you remembered a long-forgotten promise? In your reading of the Bible, you have seen forgiveness through the ages and at the cross. Still, you struggle to understand how forgiveness works. Not just here but everywhere. And there in the intersection, I wonder if I too should ask forgiveness for not being a better role model, a better Christian, a better professor, one who would have kept him out of prison. I always pray for my students. How did this one get here? Do I need a reminder of God's promise of forgiveness? I know it's there!

We talk for over an hour. The small Bible I keep in my purse is used to seek verses that remind us of God's promises, His plans for us, the necessity to commune with Him and ask for forgiveness, and to surrender our lives. I see his reaction. I see his tears, and I know there is great remorse for his chosen path. But God forgives us and walks with us and leads us to different paths. I speak of hope, the great hope we have as Christians, and the great promises we were given and claim in humility in our prayers. I speak of second, third, fourth, lifetime chances, and how we never walk alone. And I wonder, *Is any of this reaching him?*

"I made poor choices," he says. "It's like those fancy posters in corporate buildings with the nice lake, and there are ripples in the water. When we throw that pebble in, we disrupt the water. Nobody is the same. Some people start wrong and keep going. You believed in me, knew the person I wanted to be. Thank you for showing up." His lawyer knocks on the door for the officer. "I don't want you to pray *with* me, but can you pray *for* me?"

And there it is, the intersection, the Holy Spirit's whirlwind of grace blowing through our lives, reminding us …

"Endless," I say for the last time. "Endless supply of forgiveness. It's true. We talk to Him and humble ourselves. It is never too late. Choose to walk toward Him and with Him." Our eyes meet, and for the first time, he smiles. The Holy Spirit inspires a prayer I had not planned on but one that needed to happen in that space.

As he is escorted out of the room, the door remains open. I look at the mirrored wall, remembering someone is behind it. But I see the reflection in the mirror is mine, mine alone. *God, forgive me and make me a better example for those You place in front of me.*

I hear keys rattling, coming closer to my location. The correctional officer returns to the open door and nods, indicating it's time to go. I slowly stand and walk toward the door, mentally reciting over and over, *Endless forgiveness. Endless.*

For God so loved the world, that he gave his only Son, that whoever believes in him should not perish but have eternal life. (John 3:16 NKJV)

MEASURES OF FAITH

THE RED ENVELOPE CAUGHT MY EYE. THE TOP-LEFT CORNER HAS A familiar name. *It has been four months.* Setting other mail aside, I squeeze through the red envelope to see if my hands can feel the outline of a printed photograph. *She said she would send photographs.* I open the letter and smile.

Walking through the halls of this establishment, I am aware of my presence in this quiet space and place that nobody speaks of. There are no decorations. No lamps offer warm light next to comfortable sofas. Instead, there is excessive light and bars on the windows. I walk past closed doors, listening to the remains of this day spilling across the floor in front of me in sobs and whispers. It seems like these are common in a place where individuals can forget who they are and why they are there. *Sobs and whispers.* Truth be told, I only volunteer in this facility one weekend a month. I am not comfortable here. I am not comfortable watching how the mind bends. There is a certain level of spiritual delicacy in working with memory patients. A delicacy that invites you to sit, observe, and not to respond to anything that lacks logical sense. I follow individuals into the unknown for a while. *I am not comfortable here.*

At the nurses' station, I sign in and quickly walk toward

the Spiritual Care Office, hoping there is some semblance of familiar objects, people who will bring warmth back into my heart. I knock on the door and open it to find friend and chaplain colleague Lance, sitting across from the door behind a shiny wooden desk.

In the last week, I have spoken to Lance more than I had in the entire previous year. He called to ask for help. Not too long ago, an older man with a history of physical and mental illness arrived at this facility. The man carried a duffle bag of belongings and was protective of its contents. For a couple of days, the staff worked to stabilize the patient's reality. Lance requested a standard chaplain visit. The request for daily chaplain visits provided Lance with the opportunity to establish a rapport and gain the man's trust. More comfortable in the surroundings, the man shared with Lance specific details of his life. The man shared, and Lance followed up on the details. He slides a piece of paper across the desk to me. It is a list of the items in the bag. The books are mostly all Christian devotions and inspirational books. They are all books I am familiar with, books I have read several times for inspiration and grounding.

The list has a postscript: "Book wrapped in brown paper-bag strips with name 'Emma' on it." Of all the books in the duffle bag, the title of this one remains a mystery. No one has unwrapped the package. No one has seen it. The package itself is quite impressive. Great care has been taken to keep this book in pristine condition by wrapping it to prevent any damage. This detail is made clear by the extra wrapping around each corner of the package, rendering the package a "potential book." By all accounts, the information provided by the man seems to be somewhat familiar in locality and choice of literature. Research into local service communities has yielded several results for "Emma."

"I think it might be his daughter," Lance told me over the phone. "Just the way he talks about her. He remembers street signs and buildings with details that are all accurate. And then there is no last name to his own, no real idea of where he has been for the last while."

That was a week ago. Since then, much has changed.

As we walk together for a chaplain visit to this guest, Lance repeats the stories of how the man would look out the window of the room into the street. One day the man simply said, "I am so proud of you. That is a nice office, Emma." Lance thought nothing of the statement until the end of the day when, as he walked to his car, he noticed the buildings surrounding his workplace were all social service offices. Putting together names and file pieces from previous visits, Lance found a recurring contact name: Emma. The search is aided by several mutual friends, and Lance has found Emma, a social worker in the area. He has no idea why there is no contact between father and daughter and has not been able to address that fact. The book wrapped in paper-bag strips is for her. As we reach the end of the hall, Lance knocks on the metal door, announces himself to the patient inside, and we walk in.

Inside, the stranger sits on the floor, gazing at the small window high on the wall. *There is nothing here to make this place home. This is probably the most powerful visual example of solitude I have ever witnessed.* Then I see it: the duffle bag.

Lance introduces me and talks a bit about the weather and the day, letting the man become acquainted, familiar with the sound of his voice. We simply sit on the floor and wait. The man stands, methodically completing a circle of looking at us, going to the window and peering through it, sitting on his bed, looking at us, going to the window. Now we just wait.

Finally, in slow movements, the man pulls out the package from the duffle bag and hands it to me. "Do you remember this?" He places the package in front of me. I wonder if he is really talking to me. "Open it, open it. I kept it for you." I slowly open the package just in case he changes his mind. It's a book: *Famous Hymns with Stories and Pictures*. It's an old book, a compilation of old hymns with stories about the events that created and shaped each hymn. The book is very fragile. "You should play the piano again. Your mother loved to hear you play," he whispers as he touches my hand and looks me in the eye. "She loved to hear you play." Sometimes the memory of a beautiful moment cannot eliminate sadness, no matter what. "I am sorry I broke, Emma. Maybe God understood." He turns his back to us and looks out the window again.

I walk out of the building holding the book. I have carefully wrapped it back in its original brown paper-bag cover. I ponder. I have spent months searching for obvious signs of the Holy Spirit moving among us, whispering in our hearts, and inspiring acts of kindness toward strangers. In my search, I have missed an obvious place where the Holy Spirit works: our families.

The soup kitchen is welcoming. I see rows of tables filled with homeless people of all ages here for a warm meal. Emma is expecting me. *Where could she be?* I hear a kind voice: "You must be looking for me." I immediately notice our physical similarities: same height, same color of hair, same color of frames for glasses, same hairstyle. My heart breaks just a bit more. He thought I was her.

I have no words. I hand her the package. She unwraps the paper and takes a sharp breath in. Then the tears appear. *She remembers.* We talk for hours. Emma tells me her father was a concert pianist who taught her to play piano. This was Emma's favorite piano book. Her mother, a devoted Christian woman, died of cancer when Emma was a young girl. The loss seemed too difficult for her father. He disappeared for fifteen years. "I lived with a family member. They had a piano. I hated he left. I hated the anger he left inside me. You know, this book was left in my aunt's home. He must have stopped by after I went to boarding school." She sighs. "Even with *all* that, you would think I would struggle to do what needs to be done," she says, tracing the cover of the book. "Where is he?"

The red envelope contains a card and a printed photograph of Emma and her father sitting on a piano bench, smiling. He now resides in a facility close to her home. "The time left is precious. How can it be that through all these years, carrying my mother's favorite books, faith has remained strong in him? I am learning of the impact my mother's faith had in him, and now in me. Please come visit and spend some time with us at the soup kitchen! I would like to share this story with others."

I look at the card. I cannot imagine the magnitude of forgiveness offered, the necessity for gracious silence Emma has endured realizing her father simply cannot remember, so he cannot apologize. I tag the picture on my refrigerator door among familiar faces and organized lists. Searching is done. There is a careful, beautiful way in which God paves our paths together for introductions and delivery of messages. The mind might bend, but the heart is still open. They look happy. I wonder how different the music must sound for them both after so many years apart.

Therefore comfort each other and edify one another. (1 Thessalonians 5:11 NKJV)

SHOEBOXES AND PRAYERS

"My life has not been without purpose," he whispers.

I slowly look up from my reading. There's nobody else around us, so he must be talking to me. For the last twenty minutes, we have sat across from one another in the post-op waiting area of the hospital. *Should I say something?* I slowly close the book I'm reading and smile. His smile accents the wrinkles around his eyes. It's an honest smile that makes me believe there has been much laughter in his life. In his hands he cradles a shoebox with a ribbon tied around it.

He asks if I am waiting for a loved one or having surgery. I pause, recognizing a part of me feels guilty to not be the one undergoing surgery. My voice trembles a bit when I say, "I am here for a friend." He offers a sympathetic nod as if to say: *There is no need to explain.* He introduces himself. Dan.

The drive to the hospital is quiet. It's too early for anything but thoughts. I wait for my friend to say something, but it seems, just like me, she has no words to choose from. The irony is that we both teach language every day—English, rhetoric, linguistics, and communication—all the tools with which to effectively communicate. Except in a situation like this. As we reach the hospital, I hear the foreign sound of my friend's voice ask, "Do you think God heard me last night? I was praying that there would be no news of breast cancer. Do you think He heard me?"

I assure her that God heard her. There, in the early morning, we pray together. I drop her off at the hospital entrance and search for a parking space. Life can be complicated sometimes. Survivor's guilt is a powerful thing for many of us. It is for me. My friend is young, and she's a good teacher. What news will we receive?

Dan's wife, Shelly, is having a second hip replacement. He tells me the first one was very difficult. The recovery was painful. He assures me, *this* hip replacement will work. In mid-story, he pauses, pats the shoebox, and says, "That's why I brought this." I am curious.

For the first ten years of their fifty-two years of marriage, Dan remembers Shelly started and closed her day reading the Bible and praying. She would often slip little notes into a shoebox sitting at the top of the dresser. One day, he finally asked her what it all meant. She opened the shoebox and showed him the notes: an honest request for the healing of their youngest daughter, a note of gratitude for Dan's new job, a note with the word *patience* on it. The notes—strips of paper, napkins, receipts—contained scribbled statements, phrases, words, prayers, and praise, all simple thoughts of daily events. A prayer box.

"Right there in the box were endless reminders of answered prayers and evidence of blessings in disguise. There was one scribbling that kept coming up over and over." He pauses. "Notes asking God to touch *my* heart, to have *me* serve Him." Lost in memories, he gently touches the ribbon around the box. "I returned to church, went to school for pastoral training, and we served as missionaries for twenty years."

It was a prayer for purpose, a life of purpose.

The shoebox remains a tangible reminder of the strength that comes from prayer. Whether they are answered or not, our prayers are heard. Just like that, it feels like the Holy Spirit has walked through the doors and brought peace and a reminder of purpose to all of us waiting.

Two hours later, my friend is in recovery. I am ready to see her. Dan hands me the shoebox, insisting I share it with my friend. He says they have gone through many shoeboxes, and this one is for my friend. As I take the elevator to the recovery wing, my curiosity takes over. I slip the ribbon off and open the box. Inside is a three-by-five-inch card. The front of the card reads, For Today! Printed on the back of the card is a familiar psalm:

I love the Lord, for He heard my voice; He heard my cry for mercy. Because He turned His ear to me, I will call on Him as long as I live. Our God is full of compassion. (Psalm 116:1–3 NKJV)

INVISIBLE

In a small section of the local botanical gardens is a beautiful Japanese garden, complete with koi ponds, arch bridges, and cherry trees. Webbed in the beautiful scenery are meandering paths with fragile plants and flowers carefully placed behind ornamental barriers. A reminder that all that is beautiful precious often needs distance from unknown elements to thrive. I reach my destination: the sand garden. I can see the small grains of sand glisten in the sunlight. *What must it have looked like?* "But Jesus stooped down and wrote on the ground with His finger, as though He did not hear."[3] Jesus, writing, reminding humans of the frail predicament of life, accountability, and forgiveness for one another. When He was done writing, nobody was willing to cast the first stone.

How is this a story we forget? Why is it tempting to pull at loose threads, unravel someone's life by bringing that person to judgment through our actions, speech, and treatment toward them? Do we realize it? What would Jesus write on the sand today? Would we know to be grateful for what was being taught? Or would we still find stones to throw?

---

[3] John 8:6 (Revised Standard Version).

Five weeks ago, while visiting a dear chaplain mentor and friend at a cardiology rehabilitation center, I became reacquainted with an old friend. I must admit I did not recognize her. One day, as I signed into the visitor's log, I heard someone say, "Hey! I know you! We attended college together. Do you remember me? I am Andy Hunter." We agreed to meet for lunch and catch up.

The next visit, I am amazed at the story Andy chooses to pull out of her heart and place on the table. It is one of loss, a broken heart, and a deviated journey in life. It is a story that ends with an admission that one of the most difficult outcomes in her life was "losing my church family." Andy's choices and actions were weighed and judged quite heavily by others. Church friends stopped calling, and messages became more hurtful than helpful. "I felt every emotional stone cast toward me," she says. "It was an odd position to find myself in. I had to offer forgiveness to others and apologize for things I never did. I stopped attending church."

The story is familiar and adaptable. As a chaplain, I work with peers and friends who must overcome great health and personal obstacles in spaces where they should be receiving help, not reproach, from those around them. As an educator, I have often worked with colleagues who have suffered great professional and personal injuries from students who take grievances, disparagement, or personal interactions to the grand jury of online communication and social media.

Andy's story lingers in my mind. *How can I help her?* A revisit to scripture outlines the end of the story. What was said to the woman? To the accusers? And there it is, a reminder, an invitation, an exhortation to do better.

At the sand garden, I look at the plants behind ornamental barriers. Indeed, the barriers are there to keep unknown elements away so plants can grow and thrive. Are people that way? Is an unkind word or an untruth the unknown element that we must barricade against to grow and thrive? Do we thrive best in silence with God?

As the wind picks up sand and blows it away, I notice a different angle to the story: the sand. Jesus did not write on a permanent surface but rather on a malleable surface. What was written could be erased. Nothing permanent. An opportunity where grace recognized error. Can we understand that to be an opportunity to recognize our errors and fix them? A reminder that how we treat others is something we need to keep working on all the time. An open door for reflection? A lesson in forgiveness? A lesson in cautious wording?

I call Andy. I am inviting her to attend church with me. I am uncertain how her church family will embrace her, but I am certain of how God embraces us all. I glance at the sand garden one last time and remember a familiar verse:

> Let no corrupt word proceed out of your mouth, but what is good for necessary edification, that it may impart grace to the hearers. (Ephesians 4:29 NKJV)

KEEP WALKING

I CANNOT FATHOM HOW THE INVITATION CAME ABOUT OR HOW IT sounded, but the outcome is quite profound: "Enoch walked with God; and he was not, for God took him."[4] There is room to wonder about everything in this brief but detailed story for the biblical cross-references to Enoch are few. What we do have is very precious. He had a family, and he reflected God's love and character in his daily life: "for before he was taken, he had this testimony, that he pleased God."[5] His was a dedicated walk with a specific companion.

Enoch walked with God. I am intrigued by the movement in the passage: "and he was not found." Someone noticed Enoch was gone. Someone searched for him. A family member? Maybe a friend set out to find him. Whomever it was, Enoch's presence was missed. The only logical explanation for his absence was that Enoch was transferred to heaven. What an amazing exposition of Enoch's character! *Because* he walked with God, it was only obvious that he would still *be* with God.

How did Enoch receive the "great invitation"? Was the conversation particularly engaging that day? Was the company and the walk so memorable that God invited Enoch to keep walking? It may be difficult to understand Enoch's transfer from earth to heaven, but it is not difficult to imagine the relationship he had with God

---

[4] Genesis 5:21–24 (Revised Standard Version).

[5] Hebrews 11:5–6 (Revised Standard Version).

because, as Christians, it is a relationship we long for, to walk closely with God. Which begs the question: How close is *my* walk with God today?

Every time I spend a day visiting patients at the rehabilitation center close to my home, I am reminded that God will answer difficult questions and has understanding beyond our capacities of comprehension. Still, that knowledge does not prevent any of us from asking big "why" questions. Patients at the center learn how to live with mobility restrictions. It is a difficult process for the heart and body. There is a profound wisdom in one specific emotion that is common among rehabilitation patients: patience. People move past the jagged edges of a difficult situation and land in the middle, the eye of patience. The price to pay for acquiring patience is often frustration. Our independence as humans now requires dependence on someone else. It takes time. I think about this while sitting on the uneven bench of wonderment, listening to profound questions from an eleven-year-old child, Anthony, waiting for his first visit with the physical therapist.

"Why do people call it 'walking with God'?" He glances at his family, just a few feet away from us. "Pastor Sid visited and prayed I would get better and 'walk with God.' But I think he's confused. Because if God showed up, I would run with Him, not walk. God would give me a brand-new leg, and we would run!" Anthony makes a sound of what it would be like to run fast, moving his arms for emphasis. I smile. *You are already aware of the necessity—and joy—of walking with God.*

In the therapy room, I sit with Anthony's father as he watches a new reality unfold for his son. He tells me doctors are optimistic. Andrew will grow through many prosthetics and must remain active. The father wipes away tears, and I realize he is reliving the events and story that brought Anthony here. I tell him about Anthony's question, and he shakes his head.

"We are trying to keep the faith," he says. "All we have left is hope and prayer. We pray all the time, chaplain. We just pray."

Just like that, God creates an opportunity for us to talk and walk, moving through struggles of human patience and trust. The stories and events that shape a different present and future than we imagined are manageable if we keep walking. Reminding one another that we need to keep walking *with* God, regardless of the terrain. Praying that the way we journey will please Him. Praying for patience, the kind of patience that simply transforms a difficult journey into an intimate walk with a close friend.

Enoch's life pleased God, and they walked together. A similar prayer is ours: A closer walk with God, with each other. And for Anthony, maybe a little running.

I have put my trust in the Lord God. (Psalm 73:28 NKJV)

THE GIFT PACKAGE

IT TAKES US BY SURPRISE. OFTEN. IT TAKES US BY SURPRISE WHEN WE realize a prayer has been answered, but we haven't said that prayer, *yet*. It is a reminder of a greater love and care than we can possibly understand. God's unwavering love for us and attention to detail still take us by surprise. Why?

At 5 p.m., I find myself in the children's oncology ward and have the privilege to visit with a dear little friend, Mandy, five years old. Not too long ago, she had her last chemotherapy treatment. She has completed treatment, and after a long day of exams, Mandy is labeled "in remission." Her mother called me and asked me to stop by the hospital. As I prepare to reach my destination, I think of Mandy and smile. Mandy, who has a memorable laugh and always asks for hugs from the nurses, is without a doubt the happiest patient I have met. I cannot wait to see how happy she is. I cannot wait to see how happy her family is.

I open my front door and grab my umbrella. Out of the corner of my eye, I see a scarf hanging from the coat rack next to the door, a gift from my mother. I take it, haphazardly wrap it around my neck, and drive through inclement weather, searching for sunshine in Mandy's good news.

When I arrive at room 405, I see Mandy's mother putting socks on Mandy's little feet. I stand quietly, holding a teddy bear to gift to this precious child. Mandy spots me, jumps off the bed, and gives me a tight hug. I hand her the teddy bear, and her eyes light up. She immediately takes a Band-Aid from a first aid kit, places it on the bear's right arm, and explains, "I am calling it Happy Bear." as she twirls around in the room. "See? Even with a Band-Aid, he knows all will be OK, and he is happy." She laughs, and her laughter brings tears to my eyes. *Dear God, let her happiness echo in heaven, and keep her healthy and safe.*

Sitting back on her bed, Mandy is talking to Happy Bear, explaining that they are both leaving the hospital today. As we wait for the physician to make his final rounds and discharge Mandy, I sit with her mom and talk. This has been a long road for the family, and they are grateful for all the prayers and kindness shown for the care of their daughter. We pray together and talk about the future. While the future seems distant, we both know our heavenly Father will keep Mandy safe in His arms.

The doctor arrives, chart in hand, to speak with Mandy's parents, and I entertain Mandy for the moment. She is excited about going home! There are goldfish, bunnies, and flowers she needs to take care of at home. She looks forward to playing with her dolls. I hear the happy moments she anticipates and realize I need to do that more: Focus on God's gift of life and care.

The doctor talks to Mandy for a few minutes and tells her how brave she is, how brave Happy Bear is, and how the entire staff will miss her but will be so very happy she is well enough to be with her family. The doctor takes out his script pad and writes orders requiring Mandy and Happy Bear to "Go home, be blessed, have fun!" His kindness is met with laughter and hugs; I see his eyes fighting back tears. It has been a long journey to today.

An orderly arrives with a wheelchair. "Time to go home, little one," he says. "You and Happy Bear are out of here and back home!" Mandy extends her hand to me. I help her to stand and get into the wheelchair. She reaches out and touches my scarf. She tells me it's the softest fabric she has ever touched. In fact, it's beautiful!

Instinctively, I take my scarf off and tie it around her neck. "Here you go. And share it with Happy Bear occasionally."

She gently brings the scarf to her cheek. She smiles. "It's so soft. It's so nice. I didn't have one. Thank you!"

As Mandy is wheeled to the exit, nurses gather and applaud, blow kisses at her, and wish her well. She waves at them using the scarf for effect. My mother will enjoy hearing the story of this scarf!

As I arrive home, I make the conscious decision to simply run through the rain to collect my mail and then go inside. Just as I exit my car, I hear my neighbor calling out to me from her porch. She is sitting on her porch swing, safe from the rain, with a package next to her. She lifts the package and tells me the mail carrier left it at my door, and she picked it up so it wouldn't get wet. I run to her porch, and she invites me to sit for a moment. She hands me the package, and I glance at the sender's name: C. S. *Is this from my friend Carolyn?*

My neighbor hears me repeat the name and asks who Carolyn is. I tell her how I have written short pieces for the women's devotional book that Carolyn edits. We have corresponded for years, and she has become a true friend, a true mentor; she has become family. But I have never met her in person. We email, share prayer requests, and share ongoing events in our lives. Carolyn is a dear friend. My neighbor smiles in an understanding manner, and we watch the rain fall for a while.

Later that evening, in my room, I open the package and a note falls out: "I saw these and thought of you." I look inside the package. Folded neatly in tissue paper are two beautiful scarves. I touch the scarves and hold them to my face. It is the softest and sweetest material. The scarves linger on my face as I feel tears running down my face. Why am I surprised?

I carefully hang the scarves and offer a prayer of gratitude. Today I had a scarf, and I gave it away. Before I needed it, God had planned for two scarves to be waiting at my doorstep.

The Lord is good to those whose hope is in Him, to the one who seeks Him. (Lamentations 3:25–26 NKJV)

UNSIGNED APPLICATION

Growing up, I enjoyed books that began with "Once upon a time," and had blue, glossy covers of *Bible Stories* (with the word "stories" in a calligraphy font). It was a grand opening, introducing characters and plots! You had heroes and villains; there was always a favorite character to be had. With time, I have come to appreciate that stories are often necessary for purposes other than entertainment. They can be reminders, anchors for challenging times, a way for the Holy Spirit to bring comfort and connection between strangers, and divine introductions.

I sit quietly, watching Phyllis sleep. *I wonder what the next chapter of her story will be.* I wasn't supposed to meet Phyllis. The day of her accident, the county hospital in her community was full, and she was transferred here, to a hospital where I volunteered. I was hired to work full time during the weekends at the hospital. After a few weeks, I was offered a full-time position at the hospital as a chaplain. However, I received a call informing me the hospital needed chaplains two weeks *before* my scheduled start date. I was asked to sign my employment application early but hadn't done so yet. I was still a volunteer. The offer letter arrived the day I met Phyllis, and I had not signed it yet. Changing professions from academe to chaplaincy was certainly something to keep praying about. That day I met Phyllis.

To get admitted into the hospital, she had to sign "one too many documents" and worried the pen "would run out of ink." I have heard her story. She remembers snowy winters, walking everywhere because they didn't own a car (this is where she stopped narrating to introduce a new character: her husband, Larry). Phyllis was twenty years old, pregnant, working in a factory every day: "No time for vacation with a baby coming." Larry worked in a steel plant and walked her to the factory and then backtracked a mile to his job. At night, he would read from a big Bible that once belonged to Phyllis' father, while she sewed a small, white garment for the baby. "I had no idea if it was a boy or a girl, but I told Larry, we are taking this child to get blessed at church, and it will be wearing this dress no matter what."

It was a boy. Phyllis and Larry dedicated their son, Markus, to God. The handmade white garment was too long for the baby, and Phyllis used a pillow and pillowcase to demonstrate how she neatly tucked the dress to make it appear perfect. At that moment, a bit embarrassed but with a grateful heart, Phyllis prayed, "Let him grow into your service, God." Her prayers were answered. Serving as a teacher for disabled children, Markus is the music director at his home church. He volunteers in the "old neighborhood" in after-school programs, helping keep young people off the streets. His love for God and the desire to share his faith are admirable. Markus is a good son, a man who listened to the Bible stories and heard his father read from the same big Bible Phyllis had used.

I stood next to Markus as the surgeon informed us Phyllis' heart was failing. There was a procedure available to help mend her heart, but at her age, the risk was significant. The surgeons were honest about the possibility of taking on such a risk. Still, Phyllis acknowledged this procedure as one that would help her get back home, so she accepted the risks. I watched Markus hold her hand, prayer offered for them, and prayers exchanged between them. That was yesterday.

Right now, the surgical team arrives to take Phyllis to her procedure. They wait at the door as I pray with Phyllis one last time;

she reaches out both her hands to hold mine. When the prayer ends, she whispers, "Sign the application. Your parents placed you at God's feet and gave you to His service. He knew we would meet. You had a divine job application before you even knew it! It's not for man; it is for heavenly work. Sign the application. Parents, we don't sign those. We pray for them. Our children choose to sign and live out the story with purpose for God. You have been called to serve with purpose. Sign the application. You already have the job."

I watch her leave and stand silent for an hour. *How could she even know about my application? No, she certainly was speaking in general terms. She saw my volunteer badge and was making a point. I think.* I sit in the empty room, no medical bed, waiting. Hours go by, and the sun hits the room floor, keeping time by allowing shadows to dance on it at different intervals. Finally, a familiar nurse peeks through the door, walks in, and tells me what I already know: "I am sorry." She walks toward me and squeezes my shoulder. There in the empty room, I cry, conscious of the divine intervention in human experiences that become stories. God is present in every line. Conscious in this silent pain that my heavenly Father does not only see but also hears my tears. I hold Phyllis' Bible in my hands. Her father, Larry, and no doubt Phyllis and Markus held this Bible. This Bible has a new home, a new story to be part of. How do I make that introduction happen?

Once upon a time, I met Phyllis. Our brief friendship changed my life. Her stories infused me with faith and empowered me to take on challenges beyond my imagination. When she died, her family Bible was left in my care. One day, I drove to the church she called home and watched her son, Markus, lead the music service. I sat on a pew that I imagined Phyllis may have sat in during one visit. I sang. I sang for comfort. I sang for grace. I sang for Phyllis. That afternoon, sitting on the church steps, I delivered the family Bible to Markus. He looked through it, touching familiar marked paragraphs. He said it was a good Bible, and it brought him a sense of closure and renewal. *I get it, I really do.* We stood still as his tears fell close to the Bible pages. We sat together as Markus went through the books of Psalms and Proverbs and read several of the entries aloud, pointing out the marginalia of commentary his mother, his father, and probably his grandfather had written.

"Did she tell you about the application?" he asked as he smiled and opened the Bible again. "The most important job application of all: service to God. The one you sign by giving your life over to the service of God. She always used to tell me to 'sign the application; you already have the job.' The last words I said to her were 'It's OK, Mom, God is with us. I signed the application.' She smiled and seemed so relaxed. Just the day before surgery. Did she tell you about that?"

And I smiled as if it was a story I had never heard or told because it was.

Know the God of your father and serve Him with a loyal heart and with a willing mind; for the Lord searches all hearts and understands all the intent of the thoughts. (1 Chronicles 28:9 NKJV)

THE REMAINS OF THE DAY

THERE WAS NO ONE TO BLAME BUT MYSELF.

How many ways can a person waste their day away? I wonder as I hear the now very familiar chime that indicates another person is "up" to speak with a Department of Public Safety (DPS) consultant to renew his or her license. *How in the world did I let my license expire? I am number 80!* I look around the room and take note of how oblivious we are to everyone sitting around us. In the last hour, several strangers sat next to me and moved through the line with their prescheduled appointments. The gentleman seated next to me now is humming a song, repeating a phrase at random. I can't make out what he is singing. He speaks it softly and almost lyrically: "It's the remains of the day, Lord, look over us at this time, and help us know what we need to do better tomorrow for it's the remains of the day."

I casually turn just to get a glance at him. He holds a small leather book in his hands. The black leather has worn out in several places, exposing soft fabric. I recognize the golden page rims. It's a Bible. I only brought textbooks. He holds his weathered Bible in his hands carefully and artfully.

He smiles and asks, "Professor?" and nods kindly. "Is it a job or a calling?" The books I am holding give my profession away, but apparently, they also present a question about why I do what I do on a daily basis. I introduce myself and learn my new friend's name is Bill.

We talk for a moment about the importance and comfort of books in our lives. I glance at the Bible he is holding, and he hands it over for me to inspect. The invitation to look through the book is genuine, and I carefully take the Bible and inspect it as he tells me the story. He tells me it was his wife's Bible. He gave it to her when their first grandchild was born. She passed a year ago. He misses her. "But how fortunate am I to know I will see her again!" I smile. Her handwriting is found around her favorite verses. There are notes in the margins that express deep reverence and awe for promises in the Word of God. I carefully turn the pages to Psalm 91 and see the marginalia.

"That was her favorite Psalm," he says. It's a beautiful psalm. It was the first psalm I ever memorized as a child. I decide to share that detail with him, and I receive a look of intrigue. "Really? My grandchildren have memorized psalms in Sunday school, and it seems they all begin with Psalm 23. Psalm 91 is quite powerful." Bill tells me more about his grandchildren and then asks how old I was when I memorized the psalm. I sit back, remembering I was in elementary school. My mind offers me a memory. I am sitting at the table as a young child, reading Psalm 91. I can see my grandmother preparing dinner. I can hear her voice over the pots and pans and the loud stove. My grandmother tells me that Psalm 91 is about never having to be or feel afraid. It is a guarantee that there is nothing to be afraid of because God is watching over me.

"It was at a time when nightmares were common in my life," I share. "My family had moved to a new home, and the space was still unknown. What I did know was that at night, our surroundings were very dark. There were no streetlights to speak of. Not a good thing for someone afraid of the dark." I return the Bible to Bill and thank him for sharing his story with me. Bill returns to his humming. I have to know.

"I heard you mumbling or praying about the remains of the day. It's beautiful. What are you quoting?"

"It's a song, it's a song. Yes, God," he says, "it's a song my grandmother used to sing. Interesting, right, how we both have generations of faith in our lives?" Bill tells me that his days go by quickly. He is very invested in family time and in helping raise his grandchildren. "I have become curious about the people around me and what I miss. I have missed many opportunities to help others." Yet, at the end of the day, he is accountable for what he did for others with God's gift of the day, the hours in that day. "There is always something we forget or fail to see that is right in front of us to do. What would I share with my Savior about my day? Would I tell Him that I forfeit a deadline for the sake of listening to a colleague in need? Would I tell him of the homeless couple in town that needed help, and I failed to deliver any? *That* is the remains of the day. What I saw and what I did about it. What is left over, unattended but still available for us to finish and address in this lifetime." He caresses the Bible and sings softly, "Lord, oh Lord. Do not leave your people as we walk into the remains of the day. Lord, oh Lord. Look over us and be our shelter. Cover us in the stars You created. Our labor stays at the door, and the sunset reminds us of your promise and love."

I listen to his voice and the gravitas of the lyrics. It's not just a song; it's a calling. He finishes the verse, and there is a comfortable silence between us. As if we have welcomed memories into our day that remind us of the remains of this day, a reminder that we are our sisters' keeper, our brothers' keeper. A reminder of the work we are asked to complete. As if on cue, the chime indicates a new number is up. I look at his ticket; he is number 79. He is next. He shakes my hand and walks away, saying, "It's the remains of the day, Lord."

I see my friend walk away and something nostalgic about the moment grabs hold of me. It is a calling to be aware of what is left. I smile and, in a whisper, quietly finish the sentence: "Look over us at this time and help us know what we need to do better tomorrow for it's the remains of the day."

Let nothing be done through selfish ambition or conceit, but in lowliness of mind let each esteem others better than himself. (Philippians 2:3 NKJV)

LOST AND FOUND

I wasn't trying to hide. But there it was, in the form of an urgent email, evidence to the contrary. I was found through an online website where you can locate people who are supposedly lost. I didn't know I was lost. Apparently someone thought I was.

The subject line in the email read: "At last! After a long search, your friend [insert name] has found you!" I had the best intentions to reply, yet a busy schedule quickly occupied my time, and our initial communication was lost. The friend who found me sent a second message. She wanted to catch up. In a matter of twenty-four hours, not only was I lost, but I failed to respond in a timely manner.

I decided to be more proactive about staying found and keeping in touch with family and friends. Social media is a tedious task for me. It is easy to lose yourself in replies, queries, and searches. My single reply to my friend brought about an unexpected message from her. As life goes, my friend was scheduled for a business trip to Texas. Since she had found me, I figured lunch would be a benign visit and catch-up moment. She called me.

"That's a great idea," she says. "Let me give you my social handles."

Did she use plurals? How many numbers are there? Do I have enough paper for this?

"You can catch me at the 214 number, and you can text me at that number too. But if you want to send me a 3D map with the restaurant's address, send it through this number that receives texts.

That's a good alert for me. Do you have Facebook? Because we can use that as well. I think it would be lovely to post a little clip of us at lunch online. You know, our high school reunion is coming up. Email is always good. But let me give you all three of my emails. The last one is different than the email I used to find you. Sometimes I can't get into that email when I am traveling. If something comes up and you need to call me at the office, you can use the main line. They can patch you through to my personal cell. Or just text me! That goes to the first number I gave you. I won't see you for a few weeks, but if you want to chat online, we can do Zoom, Skype, WhatsApp, Teams, whatever. Let me give you my screen name!"

I scribble the information down quickly, doubtful any of it will be legible later. Maybe being found is not entirely bad, just a bit complicated. It is wonderful to speak with her, though the conversation left a collection of sticky notes containing contact numbers, email addresses, and other social handles to find my friend. I am reminded there are numerous ways to establish communication and equally numerous ways to get lost in the process. In a world of instant communication, our words are often rushed, and there is little effort to contemplate and savor the exchange.

As I look over the notes with social handles, I get nostalgic about communication. I miss the days when I could pick up the phone (one attached to a wall socket), and with excitement, hear my grandmother's voice on the other line. I miss *handwritten* letters sent in parchment paper with special stamps for the journey. I miss picking out cards for my friends when there is no special day to commemorate. When did advances in technology take away these simple pleasures? Later, I discuss the day with my neighbor as we sit on her porch swing. She tells me I am missing the point. Someone took time out of their day to look for me, she says. This is an honor.

"When I was a little girl, I would sit outside our barn at night and pray," she tells me. "We were not rich. After a long day of school and chores, underneath bright stars, with miles of nothing around me, I searched for God. No social handles, no heavy numbers. I wanted to talk to Him. I was certain He could hear me. That was my time to commune with God. I fear we've lost sight of how important communication is and how to find one another in the first place." She stops for a moment, lost in the dusk, waiting for childhood stars to arrive. "With all this modern technology, it would be unwise to get lost and forget to listen, talk, and lose the desire to communicate with the most important being in our lives who not only created us but knows where we are all the time: God." We sit for a while longer in silence, and I ponder on her words.

I realize the Shepherd didn't find the lost sheep with GPS, and Jesus didn't receive a phone call to heal Lazarus. While the timeline is far from my own, the desire to remain in communion with peers and friends—not be lost—runs deep within us. As I bid my neighbor good night, I walk the short path to my front door, and in my mind's eye, I can almost see the communication emerge. Developments in the field of spiritual communication are like a big cosmic sign, enlightening and speaking to our hardened hearts, "I found you, and I want to spend time with you. Here is my social handle: Calvary."

But God demonstrates His own love toward us, in that while we were still sinners, Christ died for us. (Romans 5:8 NKJV)

STARTING IN THE MIDDLE

EARLY SUNDAY MORNING, I AM ONE OF MANY PROFESSORS FINISHING up online course information for the new academic start. Years ago, an academic semester had a certain predictability on start and end dates. That predictability has long changed. With the great demand for online courses, dual enrollment, and the practicality of the eight-week term and weekend classes, it sometimes feels as if I am constantly preparing for a new academic start, even in the middle of one.

Having spent an entire week training on new state-mandated policies for educators, class preparation time was limited. A guest speaker from the education department provided a "Students and Online Communication," and delivered a preformatted paragraph regarding social media. That one prepared paragraph is now required in every syllabus: "No hate speech, intended violence, bullying, slander, disparagement, of peers can be posted online or any form of social media." The paragraph outlined online content supervision outside the classroom. Somehow, the fact that professors were now *required* to place this paragraph in the syllabi hurt my feelings. As a communications professor, was that not part of my ethical language choice–based curriculum, to make students aware of how language choices create or diffuse problematic situations? Complicate relationships? Hurt or encourage others?

A new academic start in the middle of a young person's life. I wondered, *Will students notice this policy? What will they learn from it?* As it turns out, I did not have to wait long to find out.

On the first day of class, walking to my assigned classroom with a colleague, my teaching colleague wish me well in a simple statement: "Time to teach." The phrase gives me pause: It *is* time to teach. In the halls, young people enter classrooms, talk to each other, laugh, and check text messages. In the last ten years, teaching has become an interesting challenge of example and practice versus academia. As Christians, do we not all teach others *every day* by our very presence, examples, and communications? There in the hall, I ask for something simple but complex: "Heavenly Father, grant me wisdom to teach well."

Minutes later, I walk around the classroom, reading through the syllabi posted on the electronic blackboard. I casually read the "online communication" paragraph, and I am quickly interrupted by a student: "Why not? What if I really don't like someone? It's my right to give my opinion, to say whatever I want. Why would the school monitor that?"

I continue to walk slowly, as if I can spot the awkward land mines now hidden all over the classroom. It's time to teach. It's a new academic start in the middle of this young student's life.

"That is a compelling statement. What about this statement should make us *all* take pause?" I watch as students wrestle with the question for a moment. What are they thinking? Do they not recognize that the state has brought forth more than just a communication matter? The state is reminding students to be mindful of their words about others. The state is reminding students to be cautious about discerning between the professional and the personal, to play nice with others, and to be kind to everyone! Apparently, teachers like me failed at teaching this one critical task!

The silence is deafening. Finally, a young woman's voice pierces the silence: "It's the Golden Rule. Not to sound religious in a philosophy class, but it sounds like what the Bible says: 'Do unto others.' How difficult is it to treat others with respect? Even if you don't like them? I am just saying ..."

I observe the reaction in the classroom as students nod in agreement and glance at the student who initiated the conversation. Our eyes meet, and he asks, "What do *you* think, Professor?"

There it is, the open door to speak of language choices demonstrative of who we are and what we believe in. An invitational opportunity—vetted in caution and wisdom—to search the obvious with students. An answered prayer and challenge to "teach well" and count on divine grace to teach what is necessary within a human space. This is where courage and grace intersect. An act of cautious courage navigated only by holding hands with the One who has asked me to always be mindful of how I treat others, no matter what. A new academic start in the middle of my own life.

The fear of the Lord is the beginning of wisdom. (Psalm 111:10 NKJV)

LIFE DETOURS

I OFTEN WONDER HOW GUARDIAN ANGELS RESPOND TO WHAT THEY observe daily—especially my angel. I never thought about it much until I began working between chaplaincy and academe. Intentional introductions keep me intrigued about the presence of the Holy Spirit in all corners of our lives.

One day, a young boy was brought into the emergency room after being trapped in a vehicle for hours. He witnessed the loss of his family. Young, profoundly brave, and intuitive, he said, "I prayed with everyone in the car. My guardian angel was there too." The event occurred years ago, but it rushes to mind when I see a family getting into a vehicle and hear their laughter. I remember and pray for their safety. I have started to call these moments of recollection a life detour. The detour is that moment when God lets me take an unexpected turn to arrive at His expected destination for my life. A tangible memory of being in the presence of the divine when the space around is steeped in mercy so that there is no doubt of "present help in trouble."

Seated in my rental car, I confirm driving directions on the GPS. It may seem strange to leave three hours early for a speaking engagement only half an hour away. However, this speaking engagement is at a university where I want to visit the library—and maybe the bookstore. I have allotted plenty of time for the drive, particularly since the weather forecast has announced potential drizzle and rain for the morning hours.

Forty-five minutes later, I do not regret leaving early. The GPS failed to indicate there would be roadwork ahead. The once-friendly navigator voice now repeats "rerouting" in an incessant manner: "Proceed to the route … Proceed to the Route." The question is: Where *is* the route? Unfamiliar with the route, I am disheartened by the next obstacle, announced by a sign reading, "DETOUR". I take the turn and decide to pull into a gas station farther ahead and ask for help. *God, please send me some help. I need some help here.* Then I hear the dreadful sound coming from a distance: thunder. The drizzle has turned into a downpour! Before I can even reach the gas station, the rain makes it so I can barely see where my detour exit is. Just as expected, the traffic slows to accommodate the rain.

As vehicles slowly move forward, I see her on the side of the road. She is holding a broken umbrella and walking away from a vehicle left on the roadside to my right. A closer look shows the vehicle has two flat tires. I watch the stranger quickly walking in the rain. *Visibility is poor. She may get hurt.* As I get closer, the thought arrives: *What if she's praying for help right now too?* Against all reason, I feel compelled to pull over. I lower the passenger-side window and try to speak over the rain, even holding up my professor identification card and assuring this stranger that I have a chaplain badge in the glove compartment. *She looks scared but relieved, maybe she was praying for help. How am I supposed to help her?*

The stranger cautiously opens the door and gets out of the rain. I slowly merge back into traffic while my new friend introduces herself. Her name is Elise. She expresses her gratitude and immediately engages on how this was meant to be a completely "different type of morning." *I can certainly relate to that.* Today is her first day at a new job. The new job comes just in time and is a blessing. But Elise says this morning has been, "unbelievably difficult." It takes us half an hour to reach the gas station. As we walk into the gas station's store she asks, "Why did you stop?"

I lack an answer, but a life detour comes to mind. One day, my mother, driving home from work, saw a lady stranded on the side of the road in the rain. My mother felt moved to stop and offer a stranger a way home. It was the right thing to do. Elise wipes away tears. "Tell your mother I am grateful. I was praying someone would help me."

That's the thing about detours. Sometimes you just remember them; sometimes you share them.

Minutes later, I have a napkin with a semi-legible map to my destination, and Elise has called for a tow truck. I glance at the slow traffic. *Will the tow truck make it on time?* I ask how far we are from her new workplace. "Not far. I know a detour. Back roads get you to the university in minutes." *University?* A new plan is made. The tow truck arrives quickly, and just as quickly, Elise and I drive down a different road on a faster route than any detour suggestions from a GPS.

"I feel like our guardian angels were working together," says Elise. "I didn't know if God had heard my prayer for help on that detour ramp."

That's the thing about detours. We never take them alone. In this life, we are guaranteed heavenly company and direction. There is this calm about the cartography of faith that resonates inside. In life's journeys and detours, we are not irrelevant to God.

Trust in the Lord with all your heart, And lean not on your own understanding; In all your ways acknowledge Him, And He shall direct your paths. (Proverbs 3:5–6 NKJV)

"PRAY FOR ME"

THERE ARE PEOPLE IN OUR LIVES WHO SHARE SIMILAR SPIRITUAL values. Among these values, for me, is the importance of prayer for each other. I have many friends who are truly fine individuals and scholars. They share very little about their lives. This is common in an academic environment, where the personal and religious are not engaged in daily discussion by any requirement. Hence, I have few friends who share their spiritual journeys and ask for prayers. I truly believe the Holy Spirit makes these introductions and, as Christians, we are called to nurture these relationships. It is a precious request: "Pray for me." Imagine all that affects and shapes your space: family, friends, work, colleagues, emergencies, daily activities, thoughts, concerns, praise. So many cares and joys to place forward in prayer. What are we asking of others when we request their prayers? Do we share specific details about where our journeys need care? What are others asking for when they pray for us?

It was my last-minute email check before leaving for work. There it was: "I read your column every month. May God continue to bless your ministry and the ministry of your colleagues. I pray for you." The sender included a citation from Colossians: "We continually ask God to fill you with the knowledge of His will through all the wisdom and understanding that the Holy Spirit gives."[6] I do not recognize the name of the sender, but humility overcomes me as I realize someone has placed my name in the presence of God, praying for my service to Him. This was quite an offer of prayer from a stranger, to lift a team up in prayer. And very humbling. It spoke of some level of inspiration that only God can provide and nurture.

Since I had collected the email first thing in the morning, the details remained with me on the drive to the university. I kept thinking, *Somehow it is important for me, today, to remember and hold the tangible spiritual gesture of an anonymous friend: prayer.* The email remains a companion during lectures at the university. During office hours, a colleague stops by my office to check in before a meeting, and we take time to talk for a few minutes. As she prepares to leave, she whispers, "Pray for me. Life is getting, well, complicated." She smiles, and then her face takes on a look of concern. Two emotions present as she feels requesting prayer is an inconvenience, but she needs it.

After she leaves, a prayer is sent to heaven, asking for special care for my friend. I don't know what is happening in her life. I know she is aware of my ministry in chaplaincy, but we never engage in theological conversation. Still, I know what church she attends. It leaves me wondering: family, health, work? *What does my friend need prayer for?* I am immediately reminded of a comforting thought: *I don't need to know. God knows. If she shares anything specific, I will pray for that as well.*

A few hours later, my friend returns from her meeting and stops by my office again. She quietly sits and shares: "I was thinking … I am aware that God knows what I need, but if you could pray for three things, things that I need to sort of, well, nurture and gain and leave up to God: strength, wisdom, patience, and …" Her voice trails off. Experience has taught me these are important requests; they are pleadings for extended guidance and grace. This request is more specific in its intent. I invite her to join me in prayer at that

[6] Colossians 1:9 (Revised Standard Version)

very moment. We spend time talking, and eventually, the focus falls on the prayers we offer for others. I mention prayer appears to be the topic of the day and briefly share the morning email experience and how important it has suddenly become to keep others in prayer. She smiles.

"I have neglected to reflect on prayers sent for me and given by me," she admits. "Can you believe that? I go to church and get a jolt of remembrance, hope, and renewed commitment. And then I get back to the everyday grind, and it's gone. I need more prayer. It has only been recently that I realized how much I need them. It's comforting to know someone prays for you to ensure your daily journey includes traveling close toward still waters."

Still waters. Peace. Care. No needs. Comfort of the soul.

On my drive home, I think about this. I do not have great wars to fight. No country comes for me. I lose sleep to personal battles; my struggles are not greater than anyone else's. I have stopped in fear while traveling the path of humanity, running through challenging terrain with trees so high the light of heaven can barely be seen. Where darkness encroaches on my life, the body remembers to push forward in faith, providing assurance that I am not alone. Still, that is its own challenge: To believe and trust in God, knowing the paths have been laid before me with great care and love.

The Holy Spirit never stops moving among us. It is part of our innate need to search for guidance in this life and for the Advocate to continually be willing to lift one another in prayer.

Still waters.

Pray for me.

For this reason, we also, since the day we heard it, do not cease to pray for you, and to ask that you may be filled with the knowledge of His will in all wisdom and spiritual understanding. (Colossians 1:9 NKJV)

OF AIRPORTS AND PHARMACIES

TRAVELING FOR WORK AND RESEARCH HAS BECOME A CONSTANT IN my life. My father, a biblical scholar and theologian, travels quite a bit for speaking engagements as well. I recently commiserated with him about all the time wasted in airports between flights. He listened and explained how he dealt with delays. "I pray and tell God, 'Here I am if I can help anyone.' Inevitably, I always have someone approach me, even about things as small as finding the right gate. You should try it." I chalk the conversation up to "someday, maybe," and my brain simply files it away.

"I am sorry. I don't know why we overlooked the prescription," the pharmacist explains apologetically. "The script will be ready in about twenty minutes, OK? Just have a seat, and I will take care of it right away."

I take a deep breath and smile. *No, it's not OK. How could you overlook a script that was submitted eight hours ago? I will sit right here in the waiting area with the blood pressure machine, in the tiny uncomfortable chair that conveys one verbal message: I am ill.*

I look at my surroundings, and for some reason, my mind wanders to the recent conversation I had with my father: "I pray and tell God,

'Here I am if I can help anyone.' Inevitably, I always have someone approach me."

Why not? I think. I take a moment to try it and say a short prayer right there. Then I sit and wait. Have twenty minutes passed yet? Maybe I should have asked my father if that prayer works for everyone, everywhere, or if it only works in airports.

"Excuse me. Spanish?"

A young man is talking to me. He does not speak English and desperately needs to find baby supplies. He holds up a coupon with a specific brand name. Together we walk through the aisles and find the item. "Gracias!" he says, smiling and nodding. He heads to the cashier; I head back to my seating area.

"Would you help me? I didn't bring my glasses and cannot make out that number on the label." The lady points at the very small print on the back of a bottle outlining the percentages of medication contained in each capsule. I help her read out the numbers.

It appears as if my surroundings have suddenly come alive! There is so much to do. There is a woman with a broken arm, trying to hold a full gallon of milk. An older gentleman has inadvertently dropped a basket of items and cannot reach down to collect them. An expectant mother needs assistance in getting the last jar of prenatal vitamins on the end of a high shelf. *I am running quick errands for others!* I smile and shake my head in disbelief. Just one prayer!

Then I see her. An elderly woman is walking toward the pharmacy counter. She looks at me and offers a smile. Every step she takes is carefully planned. Her very appearance demands no respect from those walking around her; many carelessly bump into her. She does not seem to mind. It's as if she is used to the fast-paced world interfering with the slow pace of her body. *What does she need?* I wondered. She slowly makes her way to the pharmacy counter.

"I know you don't work for me." I turn to see a man with a name badge: Brett, Store Manager. He wants to know why I've been running around the store helping customers. Do I know them? I realize that I may need this pharmacy again, so I share the details—waiting at the pharmacy, conversation with my father about the airports, and the prayer. I wait for Brett to provide that "look" indicative of, "I think you need professional help." Instead, I receive a simple, "Thank you for the reminder." *Reminder?*

As I walk back to the pharmacy, I notice the elderly woman standing at the counter, rummaging through her purse, taking out tissues and a wallet. Something is wrong. I see the pharmacist and Brett speaking softly behind the counter, inside the glass door leading into the pharmacist's office. I slowly walk to the counter where the lady is standing. I don't know what's happening, but I don't want to leave her alone, crying, standing next to magazines where there are tiny little breath mints and a significant number of candy bars. I walk toward her and introduce myself. I ask her if she needs anything. She looks at me, smiles, wipes a tear away, and simply says, "I need a miracle." Before I say a word, Brett returns to the counter and, with an apology found somewhere between a whisper and an empathetic tone, breaks the news: "This medication is not on the list covered by your insurance. Not even the generic brand is covered by your insurance. And yes, it is quite expensive for a monthly refill."

There is a pause, and she quietly closes the purse. She looks down and quietly says, "Thank you for trying."

But Brett is not finished delivering the news. "Here is my business card. I am the manager. The pharmacist has been informed of this matter, and we talked over a few options." As if on cue, the pharmacist comes up and stands behind Brett. "I am not giving you the scripts back because we can help you and fill the script. From now on, when you need this script filled, call this direct line. Ask for me or ask for him [Brett points at the pharmacist]. We will take care of this medication at no expense to you."

There is a silence, and then I hear the lady sob for a minute and again whisper her gratitude. I hear her thank Brett in a broken voice several times. She asks for no permission and simply takes his hand and slowly hugs Brett. "God bless. You are my miracle today." I step back slowly and return to my seat, ready to go back to whatever tasks await me next.

Walking by me, Brett stops, smiles, nods, and states the obvious: "Perhaps we should transform the world into an airport or a pharmacy. It appears they are two places where somebody needs help—healing, maybe a miracle." He smiles and walks away. As if on cue, the pharmacist calls my last name to indicate my prescription is ready.

Let no one seek his own, but each one the other's well-being. (1 Corinthians 10:24 NKJV)

THE GO-TO INHERITANCE

EVERYONE HAS A GO-TO BOOK, A BOOK THAT INSPIRES, MOTIVATES, and challenges the heart and mind. Whether it is a text that complements the reading of scripture, adds to what we are discovering in the Word of God, or a favorite text that brings a nostalgic remembrance of a specific time and place in our lives, the go-to book is a literary luxury that brings comfort. It doesn't matter that we know the plot and the ending. We still turn the pages in wonder.

These go-to books are easy to spot on a bookshelf as they sit, a bit more weathered than the rest, backs often cracked on special chapters, pages carefully tabbed in the top corner with a small bend at the end indicating the location of a favorite phrase or passage. Often when I visit university colleagues' offices, I take a moment to glance at the books on their bookshelves, just to see if I can spot a go-to book. Interestingly enough, the easily found go-to book is not a frequently referenced philosophy or theory book but the one often unapologetically stowed in a special place by the owner. I always wonder about the time and place and the where of how this book arrived in someone's life. I am genuinely curious about the impact it had on the person. What is it about these texts that brings us back to revisit and rediscover their content?

The phone call was brief, but the invitation extended was meaningful. Two months ago, my friend Raina's father, Dr. Page, died. A former university physics professor requested that all textbooks in his office be donated to the university library where he had worked. Raina asked, "Would you please help me pack and mail the books? It will probably take half a day." What an honor.

I arrive at the family home. Raina greets me and then directs me toward the formidable library. There are three walls with floor-to-ceiling bookshelves and library ladders. It is a beautiful office. Raina shares the story of the room. It was an addition made to the house when she was beginning her undergraduate studies. The room has cathedral ceilings and hardwood floors. It is a notable difference from the architectural style of the rest of the house. It is where her father did his research and writing.

"I have no idea where to begin. I don't want to donate something personal by accident," she says as we both admire the room.

As it turns out, everything *is* personal. The books are all in an elegant organizational pattern. Amid physics, math, science, theory books, and other scholarly texts are journals and notebooks of publications by Dr. Page. Everything is clustered into research patterns. Everything except the top shelves. At a distance, the top shelves appear to be the most used space. The books and journals mingle together. There is no clear organization. A closer inspection is needed.

I ponder the value of my friendship with Raina as I climb the first library ladder to examine the top shelves. And there they are: the go-to books. All the top shelves have go-to books, tattered copies of paperback books, some held together at the spine with tape: *Psalms, Proverbs, Songs of Songs, Job.* A long array of Bible translations follows, several copies of each. The placement of the books is as important as the words, as relevant as the content demonstrated. On closer inspection, a clear theme is presented: the search for wisdom.

As the day ends, no books are packed. The top shelves are empty, and Raina tells me stories. She remembers an array of open physics books on the desk. She tells me how her father would be working on research and take breaks from writing to read, "this red book" (Proverbs). The top shelf has yielded Bible storybooks, poetry read to her before sleep, books and words that shaped Raina's life, and words from her father that still shape her character. They all still serve as anchors in her life to discern big and little decisions. She flips through the go-to books, reading her father's notes, sharing her stories. It is clear these beautiful memories will not be packed away. These are words that were meant to be shared. Words that need to have breath for life. The lessons shared are more valuable than expected or imagined.

"I just inherited go-to books and go-to responsibilities," says Raina as we sit on the floor surrounded by books. Two small figures inside a snow globe of letters and pages swirling around us. She holds up a small Bible with several bookmarks inside it. "I can't believe I had forgotten about all of these. I grew up with these words, these promises, these important texts, and somehow, it's like reading them all over introduces me to a peace I once knew and left behind ..." Her voice trails off. And right there we pray for a blessing we feel has arrived and the pages left to be turned.

In Him also we have obtained an inheritance, being predestined according to the purpose of Him who works all things according to the counsel of His will, that we who first trusted in Christ should be to the praise of His glory. (Ephesians 1:11–12 NKJV)

STANDING ROOM ONLY

"Please do not feed the ducks."

The gentleman at the front desk places a small plastic bag in front of me but does not look up from his typing. "If you want to visit the lake area and encounter ducks, please only use *this* feed. Do not feed the ducks human food." I glance at my watch: 11:16 p.m. I will remember this as the exact time when I became disheartened. Twenty-five hundred miles from home, I am presenting at a conference in an unfamiliar city. The flight was delayed, my luggage was lost, there was an hour's wait for the hotel shuttle, and now I can't feed the ducks. Where are these ducks anyway? Probably asleep.

He hands me a conference schedule, badge, and map for the various lecture halls I need to navigate in the next two days. Stepping into the elevator, I expect a quick arrival at floor 24. Not the case. The elevator is moving extremely slowly. Exhausted from the travel, I take a moment to glance at the "Complimentary Duck Feed," noting the list of ingredients: cracked corn, barley, and birdseed. I glance at my conference badge and look at the list of its "ingredients": my name, title of presentation, and my church affiliation. I am a distressed traveler, ready to rest.

The early morning finds me in prayer, asking for guidance, aware of the great necessity of God's presence evident in these meetings. I head out to begin the day and wait for the slow elevator. Joining me in the wait is a young boy, about five years old, holding the hand of a gentleman wearing a conference badge. As we enter the elevator, I hear the boy ask, "Dad, did you bring the food for the ducks?" I smile. *He is holding his father's hand.* Doors close, a screeching noise ensues, and the elevator has come to a stop. Silence. Then I hear it: The young boy is whimpering, and it sounds like he is about to cry. The glances exchanged among everyone seem to express a mutual concern. If we are truly stuck here, will this child cry for the duration of our wait?

In one swift move, the father picks up the child and tenderly holds him in his arms. "Nothing to be scared about. It's just a little extra time to make friends."

I watch. The father has not offered a simple hug to appease the child. What is given is a genuine embrace that draws the child close to the father, who softly talks to his son, calming all fears. We are all watching this happen and have forgotten that we are stuck somewhere between floors.

"What did you memorize this week?" Still in an embrace, the father engages the young boy in conversation. The young boy begins to talk about sheep, green grass, water, and walking on a nice path with the Shepherd. *Psalm 23?* I wonder. He says the part that sticks is that they won't need anything because the Shepherd has taken care of everything. Everything!

For the next few minutes, I listen to the best sermon of the day: A child's simple rendition of God's grace, guidance, care, and mercy toward us; the gifts of nourishment and green pastures; an honest observation of the parts in the psalm that just stick. I look around and notice that everyone is engaged in the conversation between the father and the son. Eighteen floors above the lobby, my prayer for God's guidance through these meetings is answered. I feel the swift movements of my heavenly Father's arm pick me up and restore my soul.

Half an hour later, we arrive at the lobby. Nobody complains. In the first lecture hall, I sit next to one of my nameless new friends from the elevator. I see her looking through the schedule for the day.

"That was some worship service today in midair, wasn't it?" she asks. "All of us are about to speak on religious topics, and the best speaker is not listed in the program, but he filled the house! It was standing room only in that elevator!"

I look back at the lobby, wondering where the father-and-son duo are headed. It truly was standing room only. But that's usually how it goes when the Holy Spirit brings people together, and we open our hearts to life's lessons. Just like that, I decide that after the last meeting of the day, I will find the lake, feed the ducks, and celebrate the goodness and mercy that is certain to follow us today. I look at my watch, 8:01 a.m. I will remember this as the exact time, "my cup runneth over."

The Lord is my shepherd; I shall not want. (Psalm 23:1 NKJV)

TIMING IS EVERYTHING

It is often the unplanned visits, the unscheduled introductions, and the unexpected requests that make us realize how God has laid out good plans in our lives. On that Sunday, I wasn't looking for additional tasks for my day off. However, at the end of the day, I was given the most important task of all.

As my car turns the corner, I see her. Standing in the brisk morning air, holding a small black purse, wearing a light coat, hat, and gloves: Rosalie. Last night I received a call from my friend and teaching colleague Danielle. She has the flu. She says it is bad timing because she needs to take her grandmother shopping. It's a thing they do together every weekend. I offer to help. I have time. Rosalie smiles and waves as I slow the car. She acts as if we have been friends for years, when truly, this is our first meeting. As I help her into the vehicle, she thanks me for taking the time to help her run this important weekly errand and apologizes for any inconvenience. She is so pleasant! How could this be any trouble at all?

Driving to the grocery store, she pulls out a few notecards from her purse. They are wrinkled recipe cards with tiny print all over. Every Sunday, Rosalie goes to the grocery store. It is a smaller grocery store in the middle of town that has managed to survive the growth of larger commercial grocery chains around it. Sixty years ago, Rosalie's husband inherited the store from his father. She tells me it was a smaller town back then and points out crowded areas that were once open spaces. She speaks of her husband, Lance, and how much they loved the town and its people. It was a safe place, a good place. They ran the store together.

As we enter the grocery store, I can see why it is still in thriving business. It is full of people walking through aisles that are clean and beautiful. How have I never come to this grocery store? It is a multisensory experience! There are beautiful arrangements of fruits and vegetables, and the aroma of fresh bread and pastries from the bakery all hit me at once. A gentleman approaches us and introduces himself as Danielle's brother; he is the store manager. Rosalie speaks to him briefly, asks about the children, and promises to visit them soon. Then she hands the notecards to him. As he walks away, Rosalie invites me to head upstairs to the manager's office so I may view the entire store from above. The office is overloaded with family portraits and comfortable furniture. This is a second home for Rosalie. I see photographs of Danielle as a baby, of Rosalie and her grandchildren, and of Rosalie and Lance. A small love seat has a quilt with pictures of her grandchildren. This is an emotionally warm space.

Looking out the glass windows, Rosalie points to the dairy aisle and tells me that is where the weekly ritual began. Forty-two years ago, while standing here, she saw a young lady enter the store, holding the hands of two little boys. They walked to the dairy aisle. "Timing is everything. I had come to get something—I forget what—and I just happened to look out the glass windows, and something made me pause. As if my guardian angel had been instructed to tap me on my shoulder and make me aware of her. I couldn't move! I looked around and said, 'OK God, you got my attention!' I was watching her for a reason, and I didn't know why." Rosalie smiles as her gaze remains on the aisle. *She's reliving the moment.* In my mind's eye, I see Rosalie, a young woman herself, observing behind the one-way mirror windows surrounding the office, searching for the obvious. "I saw what God was leading me to. I saw it, and there was no way to imagine walking away from it. She was just a young mother, right over there." Rosalie points again as if to ensure I am following along in the story.

The lady stood in the aisle long enough that Rosalie had an opportunity to notice details. It was winter, but they had no coats. "The lady stood there with a small coin purse, counting her money, and I realized she was probably wondering how much the milk would cost and if she had enough to cover it. God had sent her my way in His time. I took a cart. You see, I had children, so I had an idea of what she would need for the boys, so I quickly shopped for her. When I reached the dairy aisle, she was *still there*. She saw me and the cart full of food. I told her, 'This is my store, and I want you to take this cart and keep filling it with anything I missed.' The lady said nothing. She looked at the cart and seemed to be silently asking, 'Is this for me?' I nodded, and she began to cry. She hugged me, and as she cried, she whispered to me, 'Thank you, thank you, thank you. God bless you! You have no idea.'

"The lady was driving to Oklahoma, back home to her father and mother, leaving her abusive husband." Rosalie's eyes tear up as she remembers her husband, Lance, joining them, putting an arm around Rosalie as if to assure her the young lady's experience would not be Rosalie's experience. "Lance and I took them to the bakery and got sandwiches, hot chocolate, and goodies for the boys." She sighs. "We gave her groceries and the little money we had. She was so grateful, I hoped and prayed. You know, she knew where she was going would be safer. She knew with children she needed to go. It was different back then, you know. She would be cared for. She would be safe." Rosalie pauses, wipes away tears, and gently tucks a loose strand of hair back behind her ear. She never knew if the lady reached her destination, reached the love of her parents who, no doubt, had been expecting her.

That experience changed everything. As the lady drove away, Lance said to Rosalie, "I am glad we did that, but we can't be doing that all the time, Rosalie." To which she answered, "Lance, do you think this store is ours? It's not. God is going to send us people, and we need to be ready. This is His store. We are just fortunate to keep it running for Him!" After that, Lance never mentioned it again and always helped Rosalie, who kept finding someone to help every week.

The weekly ritual continues as Rosalie goes about preparing notecards. Each card has a list and a location for the groceries to be delivered. For forty-two years, she has taken the time to do this. "God simply places people who need help in front of us at the right time, *His* time, and we are called to help. God's timing is everything." She points to the flower shop stand in the store. As we head toward the flower shop, I am given the most important task: to prepare a small bouquet of flowers to include in each delivery and attach a small card that simply reads: "God is good. Be blessed today."

Later that night, reading my evening devotional, I cannot stop thinking about timing. Danielle, getting the flu, was perfect timing. I had the opportunity to meet Rosalie and learn of a quiet ministry that is thriving because she has given of what she has and never questioned why. I was reminded of God's work in human hearts. And the beauty of the Holy Spirit constantly moving around us, encouraging us to look at the details, to *be* that person of hope and comfort and joy to others. The awareness we need to be attuned to the Holy Spirit's leading. I smile, imagining the stranger, the lady that Rosalie helped, drive away with her two children, bellies full, hearts renewed, a new day—a better day—awaiting her. I wonder what she was thinking. I wonder where she went. Either way, she was reminded there are still amazing people around us doing God's work of ministering to others in interesting and unique ways. Maybe she shared the story with her boys to teach them how God takes care of us. In the end, I cannot disagree. Rosalie is right: God's timing is everything.

In their hearts humans plan their course, but the Lord establishes their steps. (Proverbs 16:9 NKJV)

THE FIG TREE

They are not three Bible verses I think about often. As a matter of fact, I usually move on to other verses ahead. Yet today, at 4 a.m., during my quiet morning worship, I find the three Bible verses impossible to ignore. They have suddenly become extremely relevant in my daily life:

> The next day as they were leaving Bethany, Jesus was hungry. Seeing in the distance a fig tree in leaf, he went to find out if it had any fruit. When he reached it, he found nothing but leaves, because it was not the season for figs. Then he said to the tree, "May no one ever eat fruit from you again." And his disciples heard him say it. (Mark 11:12–14 NKJV)

As the story goes, quite a long time ago, the Savior of our world went for a walk. He had a destination, and during the journey, He became hungry. The travel companions were His disciples. Nobody had food. Suddenly, at a distance, the Savior saw a promising sign: a fig tree. *Food!* Immediately He headed toward the tree, hoping the green leaves (which truly were not meant to be in bloom yet), indicated the tree might have fruit, and the hungry travelers would be able to eat! On arrival at the tree, the Savior noticed the tree bore no fruit. No hunger would be satisfied. Then He said to the tree, "May no one ever eat fruit from you again!" I can certainly understand the curse upon the tree. Still, there is an important statement made: The Savior had an audience. The disciples present heard Him say these words. That is quite a profound statement. After all, Jesus witnessed, understood, and felt from the heart of humanity reproach, rejection, persecution, intolerance, and the tortuous evidence of sin. Humanity. When we survey the biblical text, there are many places where one's human character might provide a detailed response to an event or situation. Yet one of the strongest reproaches is for a fig tree. Jesus offered the fig tree a curse. This creates a different perspective on the narrative offering complex comparisons, illustrations, and examples to extract lessons from.

What if we explored the opportunity to reflect on *ourselves* as the fig tree? From a distance, we portray a strong appearance of potential emotional shelter and a promise of mission and ministry to others. From a distance, we serve as beacons for Christ's teachings. But how do we appear, up close? Is it truly too difficult to understand, or is it a matter of applying what we learn? For all of us who have seen the metaphorical green leaves, spent time in our life desserts, rejected, persecuted, hungry, and tired, we can certainly understand the disheartening emotion, the deflated observation in the outcome of a mirage, "This is not what I thought it would be!"

Out of season, the plant grew. Out of the time it was meant to grow, it appeared with green leaves, almost anxious to offer fruit, an unexpected blessing at a very necessary moment. Jesus was hungry. I can imagine a tired and hungry body catching the glint of green leaves, a fig tree, and turning away from the main path, just in case. Jesus went to seek the fruit. He ventured off the path to the distance only to find disappointment.

It is at this observation that the audience becomes part of the exigent moment. Why was it important to have an audience? Why was it important for those around Jesus to hear the curse placed on the fig tree? Was it just a moment in the life of Jesus or a cautionary statement of what was to be weary for centuries to come? The leaves were green. The fruit was lacking. Is the ultimate lesson as simple as to not be like the fig tree, presenting itself as useful and offering nothing of value? Is the story a call for us to be proactive in our Christian lives? How do we share with others?

As a professor, I have learned to appreciate that many of the graduate students are born leaders. However, academia challenges them to push the thin line of leading and learning. Often, students who demonstrate such promise and potential are kind. They help others. They help their communities. Other students who demonstrate that promise and potential simply have different priorities.

A colleague, Dr. Sayley, and I once commiserated on the topic over lunch at the university faculty lounge. "We have a strange job," Dr. Sayley said. "We can almost predict who will become a poet laureate, the best attorney in the area, an amazing surgeon, an entrepreneur, a difficult employee, or a combative workplace character. And we teach accordingly to provide tools for the future. But in the end, that is not what makes these students invaluable, beyond simple calculable value at any craft they choose. I often think we miss the heart of the matter over a glossy veneer of grades and evaluations. What will they really produce? What will they contribute, not just to the world, but to their communities, families, friends, and churches?"

Promise, potential, opportunity to serve. It's a call to the ministry of helping and caring for others no matter where or what we do for a living. *I wish I could share that with my students,* I thought. This is a frustration Christian professors struggle with in secular settings, the inability to bring biblical narratives into discussion. How do we present the fact that ethos does not grow on plants? Maybe I could if the story's outcome was presented, and they recognized the individual relevance. What is our takeaway? Actions matter; our actions matter! As I contemplate the necessity to share the story in a teaching environment, I realize that I have personally not seen a fig tree up close. How is that possible?

With renewed determination to wallow in complexity with the biblical text, I visit the local greenhouse store, where Kurt, the third-generation owner of the store, is a brilliant horticulturist and always eager to share stories about plants. The greenhouse store is not where you buy the beautiful, arranged flowers. You buy the seeds. There are no colored-glass vases, just pots of clay to scoop dirt into.

"A fig?" he asks as he looks through the old-style library book catalog drawer, searching for the pack of seeds. "You want to *grow* a fig tree or just *see* a fig tree? You know, those are quite interesting trees. Figs are unique in their growth process. Walk with me. I know we have one of those around here, but it is not full size. I can promise you that."

We walk to one of the greenhouses in the back, and there it is: a seven-foot Celeste fig tree. "Do you know the story of the fig tree?" I know *a* story of a fig tree.

"The story you know is a reason to walk humbly with God, to bear fruit," Kurt says as he inspects the tree. "Bearing spiritual fruit is impossible if you do not know the story of the fig tree. At least, I think it is impossible. These trees get grounded, deep roots. Something good should result from deep roots, such as strong character and kindness. This tree here only looks the part. See? It is planted in a space where the roots are limited in depth. Still, it's a beautiful tree. We cannot only look the part; we must deliver." It appears that ethos does grow on trees.

Sometimes I forget. Not on purpose, but as I wrestle to understand the divine and recognize how enormous the task of Jesus really was, coming to this earth to save. As a quiet observer, He could see what was in the hearts of everyone he met. This must have been agony. Something innately human tells me that He probably encountered many fig trees in human form. In my professional engagements, in my personal life, in my chaplaincy appointments, I have seen this phenomenon. I am certain everyone has seen and felt the loss of falling short of the expected, of not being able to deliver what is asked of us. How do we engage this topic in an honest, self-reflective, and self-accountability moment? How honest can we be with ourselves about what we *are* doing and what we *should* be doing? As my dear friend Kurt stated, "We cannot only look the part; we must deliver."

Back at the university faculty lounge, I see Dr. Sayley and approach him with a gift: the seeds for a fig tree. He looks at the seed packaging and smiles. "This is interesting," he says without really engaging in a formal observation of the seeds. We sit down and develop an interdisciplinary workshop for our students: introduction to horticulture as a base for a conversation about ethos and decorum. Will it work? We don't know. We sketch out the proposal for the dean of academics. It does resonate with the rhetorical canon, so why not send it forward in faith? In that moment, my colleague recognizes and reminded me about what we do—or hope to do—in our classrooms all the time: to inspire curiosity toward the use of academia for the sustenance of service to others. "Dr. Rodriguez, let's help these seeds get planted."

I am the vine; you are the branches. He who abides in Me, and I in him, bears much fruit; for without Me you can do nothing. (John 15:5 NKJV)

EXPLORING GOD'S ECONOMY

What is the most difficult experience you have gone through? How many struggles have you survived? Have you witnessed events that shake your faith? Do you remember that feeling of despair when there was truly no obvious outcome to an impossible situation? Have you ever crumbled to your knees only to cry and discover our mortal language has no word to properly describe the despair you felt? And yet, God hears your plight. Has scripture not shown us that God is a God of graciousness, mercy, and abundance? When we recall those experiences, is it easier to see how God had a hand in our journeys.

"It takes an unreasonable persona to dismiss 'God's Economy,'" says the inspirational speaker. As if on cue, everyone who was marginally awake has now woken up. Including me.

Sitting through a required pastoral care workshop, I am listening to the last guest speaker for the day. She has used a familiar term: "unreasonable persona." Just yesterday, in a persuasion course, I shared this term with graduate students. An unreasonable persona is someone who simply refuses to engage in dialogue about a topic; someone who has missed important details that would otherwise help him or her make an informed decision or observation during a difficult situation. The difficult concept of an unreasonable persona is the fact that we often fail to recognize the characteristics of an unreasonable persona in ourselves.

I listen to the inspirational speaker say that all experiences Christians go through are meant to prepare us for the next moment, for *this* moment. She explains that God has witnessed our tears and our joys, and He has been part of our journeys. "Nothing in our experiences goes to waste," she says, "No emotion, no event. Our experiences are all a blessing, even when it is a painful or hurtful experience. Our pain is a recycled blessing from God." Pain? Recycled? I have officially become an unreasonable persona. Honestly, I am uncertain why I feel apprehensive to accept such a strong statement. After all, I know I serve a loving God, not one that engages me in pain. Right?

As the speaker continues talking about recycling blessings, I glance at my colleague, Mike, who signed up for this workshop to meet continuing education requirements. Both of us are delinquent in keeping up the required continuing education workshop hours for the quarter. As the speaker continues, I note Mike's clenched jaw and tight grip on a notepad and pencil. Unreasonable persona?

The ten-minute break arrives, and I follow Mike to the reception hall, where refreshments await. *Something is bothering him. Something is bothering me.* In my experience attending conferences, I have learned to approach ideas and phrases with caution. Personal ideologies are often nothing more than that, personal and not based on anything other than opinion. But there was something about this speaker that was difficult to connect with and simply chalk up the ideas to her personal ideology.

As we walk around the reception hall, Mike confesses the speaker's message has created turmoil in him. After spending six years abroad, fighting in a war, Mike cannot reconcile the notion that God has "recycled" any emotions and experiences for the right now. "Even when hindsight is 20/20, is it not easy to find or affix a potential blessing to something that happened to us? A difficult experience gathers meaning when we are no longer *in* it but can speak of *it*."

As I listen to him, I am aware of the struggle with the individual words used to make this potentially problematic statement. I think of how God's economy has played in my life. If nothing goes to waste in God's economy, does He allow the terrors we inflict on each other as human beings to happen and simply encourage us to recycle the experience and share it with others as a cautionary story? Terrible things happen, and we often ask why. Has the answer finally been found; "It's simply God's economy." Many times, God has picked me up from locations, jobs, situations, relationships, and places, and even though it is not obvious at the moment, I am planted in greener pastures. That is a different experience, though. Right?

"God's economy." Why is this phrase bothering me so? Is it possible because we sound like a commodity in this cosmic plan and not a valuable servant of choice?

On my drive home, I can't shake the lecture. There is wonderment inside of me as I observe how God makes plans, provides the necessary introductions, and reminds us that our daily labors must include Him. There is awe because all of this is good. To have a humble spirit and be able to ask God to spend the day with me is humbling, and it is a gift. Yet there is wonderment because I sometimes forget how careful my God is with my self.

Later, at home, I am ready for much-needed rest. The phone rings. It is Mike. He tells me that on the drive home, he remembered something that made him think about God's economy. "I was in a hospital, injured, and the medical team had already told me I was going home. I remember long days of excruciating pain. I had three back surgeries and both knees replaced. I had never felt such horrible pain as I did with bone surgery. The bones that were meant to keep me walking tall, defending, running to help others failed me by breaking and leaving me injured. I was in a dark place. During that time, all I had was a Bible the army chaplain left with me. I read it cover to cover. It was my lifeline. I am telling you, I would not have made it had that Bible not been given to me. That's when I decided to become a Christian. That's when I decided to become an army chaplain myself."

There is silence on the line.

"Maybe it's not about God's economy, but instead, God's continuing education for us, like the one we went to today. It is often in the least of all places that we find Him and are reminded about our experiences. This brings us closer to God. Do you understand? Honestly, tell me what you think."

I recognize Mike is appreciating how his walk with God is now informing the choices he makes and how he moves forward in life. I encourage my friend to pray over these reflections. It appears there is not much to say but much to recognize that as Christians, we struggle with the many unexpected questions and timings of situations. What we know for sure is that we can rely on God to be present with us in His time. We just need to remind each other of that constant presence. It is not just a lesson to rely on but a gift received, paid for by Jesus Christ at a high cost.

God's continuing education? No unreasonable persona here.

For He Himself has said, "I will never leave you nor forsake you." (Hebrews 13:5 NKJV)

WANDERING IN GOD'S WONDERLAND

THE BACKPACK IS TWO POUNDS HEAVIER THAN EXPECTED.

"Take something out and reweigh," says the tour guide, casually placing the backpack in front of me as if this were not a problem but a small inconvenience. He quickly calls out for the next person in line.

I am about to begin a climb I did not search for but rather volunteered to join as a favor to a friend. The request was benign: "I am taking the graduate MFA team of creative writing students to the canyon for a writing-intensive escape. I need another faculty member and thought you would love the canyon! You haven't been there yet."

That was three weeks and two pounds ago. Standing at the entry of our trail, preparing to "gear up," I am questioning just how incredible this canyon *truly* is. As I look around, trying to find my colleague to request assistance with the emptying of my backpack, a familiar student walks toward me and simply lifts my backpack, pressing on top of it, shifting the contents in a casual manner. He quickly identifies the problem: too many water bottles. In a quick motion, he unzips the backpack, removes several bottles, and reweighs the artifact. Perfect! The water bottles are placed in the "this will not travel with us" bin. The student explains that two pounds will feel like ten pounds in a few hours. Yet, I am not convinced water is what

I want to leave behind. "The trail has areas of fresh water to refill canteens. Don't worry. You don't hike much, huh?"

I shake my head and catch a glimpse of the sunrise that suddenly outlines the sketch of the dangerous—but curious—trails ahead. The student smiles. "Welcome to wonderland," he states, pointing to the variety of trails I may choose to traverse. Just like that, I enter multiple spaces and narratives.

The room is quiet, too quiet. I stand in a corner of the atrium and observe as students walk toward the auditorium door, scan their student identification cards, and wait. They wait for the red light above the door to turn green, confirming the "system" recognizes the student and grants entry into the computer lab. Somewhere on campus, a computer has determined this student is in the right place at the right time and has submitted all proper documentation to take a graduate school entrance exam that will determine successful entry into graduate studies.

Today, along with three other colleagues, I will observe student progress on a screen in a separate room. The screen allows access to view every question a student answers in the next six hours: mathematics, vocabulary, science, and a writing sample. I represent the writing portion of the exam in case there are any questions by students or evaluators. As I take my seat next to a mathematics professor and friend, I glance at the proctor's red book, which outlines the questions for students by category. I point at the initial terminology on the pages of math questions: "extreme value theorem," "Newton's method," "Rienman sum." I shake my head and admit the math section would be a guessing game for me. My colleague laughs and turns to the last page of the book, where one of the writing prompts is located.

"Do these students know who they are?" He points at the essay question. "This essay option is an autobiographical essay. Experiential material. That's a tough one. How do you grade that? How do you give points based on someone's life story?" Suddenly, the math questions appear simpler than I imagined. In them, there is a level of calculation, formula, margin of error, and correction not available in autobiographical writing on the spot.

"We don't grade it," I whisper. "We cannot evaluate someone's personal story. We evaluate the process, organization, grammar ..." I hear my voice trail off as I notice a student in the back row, head down. *Is he praying?* I wonder. Suddenly, the screens light up. The exam has begun. I look at the clock. There is not enough time to write that essay, not as a student or a professional.

The story is one to remember. A girl wandered off and found herself in an unknown space, in a curious place, where all she could do to remember who she was required her to repeat memorized poetry. Her oratory, the language, and organization of the poem gave her the comfort of knowing who she was in this strange, new environment. Memory and delivery validated her identity. Until she forgot. The poems became confusing, and the delivery became difficult. The girl walked through a garden alive with funny creatures and unique characters, all the while learning and observing so many new things that the original content—the language and the poetry—was no longer intact or accurate in her memory. When the moment came to identify herself, Alice did not know who she was:

> "Who are you?" said the Caterpillar.
>
> This was not an encouraging opening for a conversation. Alice replied, rather shyly, "I—I hardly know, sir, just at present—at least I know who I was when I got up this morning, but I think I must have been changed several times since then."[7]

[7] Lewis Carroll, *Alice's Adventures in Wonderland* (New York: Macmillan, 1920).

I cannot engage in any analysis or image of Alice other than the one I find in the original text by Lewis Carroll. A critical analysis of the book engages the complex, dangerous exploration of the nature of language, communication, and yes, philosophy. It is at the core of this book that my curious mind—as a professor, a friend, a writer, a daughter, a chaplain, a sister, an editor, a Christian—takes a walk, a quick life review: Who are you? Alice is not simply confused about her identity and presence in a new space, she admits to something very powerful: change. "I cannot go back to yesterday, for I was a different person then."[8] I can relate to the reshaping of self, considering unexpected life situations. I do find Alice to be a bit braver in her understanding of the impossibility of going backward when she is now a different person. Has anyone else noticed this difference?

In moving forward, the things we have etched into our hearts, memorized, and carried with caution often expand or shrink. The lessons we learn affect others. How do our changes affect the relationships we care about: friendships, family, church? With so many changes in our personal wonderlands, it seems wise to nurture the roots of faith to remain grounded in them. Yet Alice's words linger in my mind: "I cannot go back to yesterday, for I was a different person *then*." How fragile or accurate is change in our daily lives? Do others recognize a different character in us, one that is exemplary? Or do we only wander through our tasks without contemplating how our presence affects others' journeys with God?

The first question encountered by humanity was not one of identity but of location. It was not a complex linguistic feat. It was a simple question with devastating realizations woven through each syllable: "Where are you?"

Of all the questions asked, this one is often posed out of curiosity and fear. Have you witnessed a mother call out to her child who is no longer standing next to her? When a response is not immediate,

[8] Ibid., 28.

the mother's tone and action change rather quickly and passionately. There is a desperate, devastating transition of a human voice running through rungs of emotions: curiosity, anger, fear, desperation! "*Where are you*?"

These are *our* human emotions, ones we recognize. Our limited human emotions. Consider how it must have sounded for the Creator, aware of the events that occurred, to walk into the garden and ask, "Where are you?"

> And they heard the sound of the Lord God walking in the garden in the cool of the day, and [they] hid themselves from the presence of the Lord God among the trees of the garden. Then the Lord God called to Adam and said to him, "Where are you?" So, he said, "I heard Your voice in the garden, and I was afraid because I was naked; and I hid myself." (Genesis 3:8–10 NKJV)

Compassion. Unfiltered, genuine compassion. Extended compassion where the omniscient Creator invites those created in His image to explain what has happened. The words narrate a terrible judgment of character, an error that will cost everyone present everything! Compassion toward a being that is now naked, vulnerable, fatally wounded. More than a ripple in the water, the weight of the stone in this failure to obey has caused a cosmic ripple. Yet nobody is forgotten. The Creator searches for the creation, and there is compassion. "Where are you?"

After that day and to this day, I struggle with the same question of where I am and who I am because the struggles are many. Because my memory is short lived. I forget the miracles passed, the promises written out for me. I negotiate the trails passing gardens, deserts, and canyons, seeking, though often not ready to admit that I already have what I am searching for! I just need to embrace it and demonstrate it: more compassion toward others.

What would it be like if we could avoid the lingering questions of identity by acts of compassion? What would it take to shake away apathy? How has it occurred that we often engage in living the example of Jesus's life and ministry and forget that compassion toward others is a vital part of that ministry? Do we simply assume loving one another demonstrates compassion? Or does compassion drive us to love one another? When my emotional and spiritual wanderings take me to the edge of the page—where I am asked to write out, speak out, and acknowledge who I am by the method of narrative and action—it is a bit frightening to acknowledge that I am different today from yesterday, but my faith walk continues to move forward, walking in grace, walking with a purpose and a direction.

After eight hours in a small room, observing students work through examinations and signing documents to push the data forward, I am happy to walk out of the building. The weather is relatively pleasant, and the sun is just bright enough to invite a moment of respite at the university courtyard, an invitation to sit down and take in nature if just for a moment. In the courtyard, there is a fountain. It is an old fountain that is subtle and poignant, perfectly placed between the science buildings and the arts building. I often wonder if this fountain, "hears" less from those around it than it should for it seems that nobody ever sits around the fountain. Never have I seen a gathering of friends at this fountain or heard a conversation around the monumental sculpture raised above the water. I wonder if friends gather here at all, sit together on the edge of the water, and discuss important topics.

The good Samaritan is the image in the middle of the fountain. In a place where education for the future is offered, this fountain offers wisdom in the form of visual rhetoric. It is not *just* a structure; it is a strong statement. A reminder of what you cannot teach but hope to witness students learn: kindness and compassion.

As I walk around the fountain, I make an abrupt stop. A young man sits quietly, staring at the pavement, hunched down, elbows resting on his knees, and a backpack next to his feet. *I know you. You were part of the student group that took the exam this morning. You were the one praying.* He looks up in surprise.

"How are you?" I ask. "You had a busy day."

"Yes, ma'am," he says, standing up. I shake my head and tell him I do not wish to interrupt his thoughts. He is the first student I have seen sitting there in the eight months I have worked at the university and lived in this new state. He tells me that he never has time to visit this side of campus but has a fondness for the fountain. "It's inspiring," he says pointing at the images. "He knows where he's going. He saw a broken man in need; he helped a stranger. Showed compassion, no questions asked." We speak for a few minutes. He shares that he has a full-time job and goes to school full-time. Pursuing graduate studies is a goal for him. As I wish him a good day and walk away, he calls out, "Professor, how long until I know what my score is?"

I explain the exams are graded by a professional team across the nation who receives the exams electronically. The team never meets the students. It will be weeks before that team is done with the exams. He looks worried, so I change the topic for a moment and ask about his job. He works as a tour guide at a national park close by. He tells me how his job was an answered prayer.

"After high school, I was not in a good place," he says. "I had to spend some time in rehabilitation for substance abuse, and my family and I were at odds. A friend of the family hired me for this job, no questions asked, at the national park, cleaning up some areas. I started getting there early in the morning to just be alone and think. I started praying again. Got back into school and getting good grades, thank God. Things changed." He looks away as if the last portion of his story is heavy, and he doesn't want to hand over the weight. Noticing a pattern in his storytelling, I tell him that early morning prayers are important and encourage him to keep the faith and remember how important it is to show kindness and compassion, no questions asked. He smiles and tells me about his job.

"At my job, there are some evenings when the stars are so bright, you have no doubt God is watching. I would love to reach out and touch them. I think it would be like touching faith. It's like a wonderland out there. Somehow in nature, there is compassion, no guilt. You just reminded me of that word, *compassion,*" he says. "Maybe one day I can grab a star, keep it safe, and have faith with me all the time, all the time."

A shining star of faith. No guilt. That sounds like a fine idea.

As I walk to my office, I think about the fountain. Maybe it is not just a display of kindness that is demonstrated by the good Samaritan but also compassion. I do not even think about that word much on any given day. There are topics I think and speak of quite often: sacrifice, timing, prayer, wisdom, forgiveness. Why has compassion been long omitted? Do I believe it is secondary or added into other words and actions without any need of explanation or awareness?

Nature is a keeper of identity and time, filling the pages of our life passports with stamps of awe, experiential learning, and appreciation for scenery too exquisite for words. As I watch the sunset at Bryce Canyon National Park, Utah, unencumbered by longitude or latitude awareness, I stand at the edge, amazed at what I see. I am surrounded by awkward jutting structures that speak of careful architecture and precise stone cuts to sit and listen to the loud silence of nature. I have followed jagged edges for climbing in no straight line or form toward a higher space simply to witness *this.* As my gaze slowly takes in the horizon's details, there is simply no denying that this is inexplicable. Truly a divine wonder.

I see the deep-blue evening sky and stars slowly drip over the sunset canvas as the wind carries parting words of birds and places them at my feet in small swirls of dust that linger and leave faint echoes of songs reverberating through towers of stone. "What is man that you are mindful of him? The Son of man that You visit him" (Psalm 8:3, 4 NKJV). How appropriate that in this moment of just God and I, there is no question of who I am, where I am going, what I remember, where I have been. At this moment, all is well. My soul is at rest. My mind is not consumed by deadlines, language, appointments, or questions. I am simply grateful for the compassionate kindness of a Savior who cares for me, for us. For all the blessings, the daily awakenings, the divergent paths, and the limitless painted skies remind me of grace and compassion.

From the corner of my eye, I see the familiar face of the student, the one who helped me repack items for the journey, the one who recognized his own journey and shared it as we stood next to the fountain on campus not too long ago, with the shadow of the good Samaritan falling near our conversation. Tonight, he guides many through these amazing skies. Somewhere on his own path, he learned to stop and reach toward the heavens. And it makes me smile as I see him extend his fingers toward the sky, as if conducting an invisible orchestra of stars. He knows of the joy of knocking on the sky, feeling the texture of faith and wandering in God's wonderland.

Direct my steps by Your word, and let no iniquity have dominion over me. (Psalm 119:133 NKJV)

BREAKING BREAD

I HAVE LEARNED A VALUABLE LESSON FROM MY FATHER. HE ARRIVES at work early, very early. Always before the rest of his team arrives. There is a silence in that space that is quite precious. I remember asking him why he did this, and his answer was simple: "It is a good time to commune with God, share my plans for the day, ask for guidance, and, of course, it's a good time to write."

My academic semester workdays begin at 6 a.m. Classes begin at 9 a.m., but in the quiet of the office suite at 6 a.m., I find it a truly beautiful time to commune with God.

Then came Joel.

Monday, by 5:45 a.m., I have turned on all the lights in the office, turned on the hot water carafe, and made sure that there is an assorted array of beverages for the day in place. I share an office suite with four colleagues. Our office suite is situated where there is heavy traffic from students every day. We all decided we wanted to have a beverage bar for our students. Not all students can afford to visit the cafeteria to pay for a $6 orange juice bottle. As a community, we all chip in and keep the office stocked. As we work, we *sometimes* hear students walk in and get a cup of hot water for their tea or grab a water bottle; it depends on what they need. But we *always* hear them say, "Thank you, professors." My office suite colleague and math professor, Heather, says, "It's not the 'thank you' that warms my heart. It's the fact they appreciate what is given to them."

Students come and go and say thank you. But Joel broke the routine; he engaged in conversation.

Sometime after 6 a.m., I sit at my desk, grading essays. I have committed my day to God and prayed in my office to be an instrument for His work.

"Excuse me?" I hear a weak voice outside the office suite door. "Excuse me, is anyone here?"

I open my office door to see who is visiting at this hour. The student introduces himself as Joel. He is carrying an overloaded backpack, wearing glasses, and looks a little apprehensive. He is holding wrinkled money. I introduce myself and ask if he needs help.

"I only have $1.31 today, and the cafeteria asks for more than that for orange juice. I was wondering if it would be okay if I could take one of these and bring you the money difference tomorrow?"

What?

I tell him that the beverages are his to take; there is no charge. He looks at me and then looks at the money in his hands. He tells me he would feel better if he could pay for the juice. I insist and even invoke the tradition of starting the day by sharing with others, breaking bread with one another, and hospitality. I smile and gesture for him to take anything he wants. He slowly places the money in his pocket and grabs a juice. I am missing something. I can feel it.

Joel grabs a napkin and a granola bar. He pauses before grabbing two more granola bars. He says thank you at least five times and then out of nowhere, I hear myself ask, "Have you had breakfast?" *Where did that come from?* Joel looks at me, holds up the orange juice and granola bars, and says that is his breakfast. He never has breakfast because he works the night shift, and there is never time or money. There is something innocent and real about his response. This is the reason my peers and I have maintained these items for students. The early morning classes are mostly populated with students who arrive in fast-food restaurant uniforms, or shirts with company logos. They work the night shift and take the first class before going back home … or sometimes back to work. I can barely hear the last part of Joel's reply. I grab my keys to lock the office and invite him to the cafeteria. He looks at me and puts the juice down. I tell him to bring the juice and add that I have not had breakfast myself, and today is a ten-hour day with no break! In truth, I never have breakfast at work, but here we go!

At the cafeteria, I select a few items and tap Joel's tray with a spoon, insisting he get more food. We gather carryout items, and I watch him prepare three paper bags at the checkout and quickly help him with utensils. Three breakfast bags later, we walk back to the main hall, and Joel, who walks next to me, thanks me repeatedly. I wish him a good day and head back to my office while Joel stays in the common student area. I have a feeling he might appreciate a quiet breakfast on his own. As I walk past the beverage bar in the office suite, I think about all the students in the college. Why Joel? I recount the interaction and pray for the young man I have just met. I still wonder, *Why the early introduction, God?*

An hour later, I walk out of my office, headed to class, and in the distance, I see something interesting: Joel with two other young students. I cannot hear them, but I am quickly reminded that kindness is often gifted in silence. Joel is opening the breakfast bags and sharing his breakfast with the other students. He's sharing *his* food. What he doesn't let go of is the orange juice he acquired in our office suite. He waited. He waited one hour, hungry, to share his food with people he cared about. I watch them sharing with one another, smiling, opening textbooks, and moving notebooks into backpacks.

As it turns out, breaking bread together is good for the soul and the heart. I smile in gratitude that the Holy Spirit always brings about the introductions. I quietly slide the glass door of the suite shut and head to class remembering.

But my God shall supply all your need according to his riches in glory by Christ Jesus. (Philippians 4:19 NKJV)

ORDINARY PEOPLE

THE BEST PART OF PUBLIC TRANSPORTATION IS THE RARE opportunity to sit back and observe everything around you. There is no concern about speed, starts, and stops. It is just an ordinary journey to a familiar destination. Then again …

As the metro train stops mid-rail, lights flicker, and I question my choice of transportation. Today I travel to the city, and it *appeared* prudent to take the train and exit at the street across from my destination instead of driving for two hours. An overhead announcement alerts passengers to remain seated. We are next to the highway, distanced from rushing cars. It's just a delay, not an end to the journey. I have time for a delay.

I look around at my fellow travelers. Much can be discerned about someone's profession and what their day may look like simply by the clothes and items they carry. *I wonder if anyone can tell what I do for a living.* Probably not today. I have a presentation today. I am presenting a grant proposal to fund a clean water project abroad. I glance at my watch, again, and pull a small notepad from my purse. I read over the main points, research, necessity, and finances requested for aid. *Dear God, help me persuade the committee to provide aid for this humanitarian project.*

Around me, my traveling companions slowly become restless. A little girl crawls on her mother's lap. Our eyes meet as she wraps her arms around her mother's neck, embracing her mother. "I am thirsty,

Mama," she whispers. Her mother explains they will be home soon. The girl hides her face. A small paper bag in my purse contains two small water bottles, visual aids for my presentation. With a quick explanation, I hand them to the mother, who thanks me. As I watch the child quench her thirst, the task ahead becomes obvious: She is not the only thirsty child in this world. God provides for His children, and He inspires His children to help one another.

In a few seconds, the train moves forward.

Inside the building, my destination is floor 25, conference room #5.

"Good morning, ma'am. What floor?"

The elevator has arrived and a gentleman wearing a uniform matching the colors of the lobby décor stands waiting for a response. As we begin the journey, he smiles and offers me a bottle of water. *Water? Is this the theme for today?* I accept the gift. As the door opens, the gentleman points to the conference room. "I wish you well in your presentation." I imagine he knows what every conference room is used for and gives his kind words no critical analysis. As I walk down the corridor, I pray for the Holy Spirit to touch the hearts of all who can make a difference today. Then I step forward.

Four hours later, I wait. I will know the outcome of my presentation when I arrive at a meet-and-greet gathering inside the lobby reception room this evening. As the elevator doors open, I see him again; the same gentleman is manning the elevator. This time he doesn't ask where I am going but simply presses the lobby button. As the elevator doors close, the gentleman shares an unsolicited story.

"I grew up in a place where we had to work hard to make water drinkable. A day did not go by when I did not realize how important it was to have clean water and how important it was to preserve clean water. Every day, I would help my mother boil and treat water." He pauses. "For many years now, I have helped ordinary people reach their destinations here. I watch, listen, know why they come. I believe ordinary people accomplish extraordinary things if guided by God's grace reminding us not to forget where we came from and to move forward, help others. Sometimes it's a thirsty village or a thirsty little girl on a train." He looks at me and smiles. "I was on the same metro train as you this morning."

The elevator stops, and the doors open in the lobby. He points toward the reception room. My travel companion hands me another bottle of water and smiles. "Congratulations on the grant. God will bless His ministry." The elevator door closes. I look at the water bottle. Ordinary people, humbly invited to work in God's extraordinary projects. That's just the way it should be.

But when you do a charitable deed, do not let your left hand know what your right hand is doing, that your charitable deed may be in secret; and your Father who sees in secret will Himself reward you openly. (Matthew 6:3–5 NKJV)

HEAVENLY STARS

It is 3:12 a.m. I cannot be late. I have made a promise to my friend Leslie that I must keep. As I pull into the hospital's oncology facility, I remember a picture Leslie drew about five months ago. She had drawn the hospital in intricate detail, and angels surrounded the building. One angel was looking out her bedroom window. All the angels were smiling. Leslie was quick to explain that the angels didn't stay there all the time. She said that some left with me and went to my house. She once said, "I tell my angel it's OK to drive home with you and make sure you are OK." What a poetic thought.

Security officer Allen greets me at the door, smiling as he walks by, probably to ensure the front doors have locked behind me so we may be safe again. He is always smiling, and his laughter is more powerful than any security measure he could ever use to keep patients out of harm's way.

On the second floor, I find Leslie sitting on the side of her bed. She is dressed in a light blue sweat suit and untied white sneakers. She is sitting next to her mom, who is placing a warm cap on Leslie's head. She looks up and smiles. And I remember why I dragged my tired body out of bed. I kneel in front of her and tie her shoelaces as she lists galaxies and stars. Today we will sit on the bench outside the hospital and watch the stars disappear as the sun comes up. Sneakers laced up, I squeeze Leslie's little shoes and tell her it's time to go. She waves goodbye to her mother, who will watch us from the room window. Leslie extends her little hand up toward me. She does not ask, but I know she wants me to hold her hand. I do.

As we walk, I realize the terrain is difficult. Leslie points at the lake, clapping her hands and asking me to walk faster. In my mind's eye, I can see Leslie running ahead of me, full of energy and life, splashing into the shallow end of the lake and scaring the ducks. But the truth is, she lacks energy.

Ten minutes later, we have settled on a bench close to the lake, and Leslie is pointing out every star we can see. How long has it been since I have seen the stars? I watch her little fingers point at the heavens. She calls them "God's stars." As the sun peeks over the horizon, she rests her head on my shoulder. She is already tired. I put my arm around her, and she asks, "Are we stars? Do we shine?" The question makes my eyes tear up, and I quietly sit as tears run down my face. In the early morning dew, I know the Holy Spirit is settled with us, helping us to understand the beauty around us is a gift, and the time spent with one another is a blessing. Before I can answer Leslie's question, she falls asleep.

Do we shine? I smile, remembering the old familiar song "This Little Light of Mine" I look down at the small child resting, undergoing such grown-up treatments to stay alive. She *is* a star. God is present, helping her to keep shining. The thought strikes me that this child, undergoing such a physical challenge of illness, still wanders through God's creation, amazed and curious at all that is around her. Everything she sees, she credits to God. It's not a small reminder but a rather profound thought: Anything good in this life and everything beautiful in nature must come from heaven. All this time I thought we were looking after her, but Leslie has looked after us.

There is something humbling and sacred about divine compassion and how the Holy Spirit reminds us of it, encouraging us to look after one another, care and love one another, shine in places where darkness may reside, and remember that God is always present. Still, to shine? How do we do this? Is it about visiting the ill? Waiting on the side of the bed, unable to tie your shoelaces, yet still being happy and trusting God will bring someone to help? Is it recognizing the wonder of the cosmos, amazed at God's creation? Is it the silence between us that needs no explanation because there is love, sympathy, and empathy in our hearts? Is it the comfort of holding your hand, knowing there will always be someone to take it and hold it tightly through any terrain? We are all patients of sorts. Jesus identified Himself with the suffering of humanity to provide the final solution. Caring for each other, this we do as we witness the consummation of the work of hope and deliverance He initiated.

The sun is coming up. It is time to go. I hear someone approaching us and see Allen bringing a wheelchair. I am grateful for his kindness, thinking ahead to how we will return Leslie to her room. I tell him Leslie has reminded me of a childhood song, and just like that, in a whisper as to not wake Leslie, we sing the song together all the way back: "This little light of mine, I am gonna let it shine."

And whatever you do, whether in word or deed, do it all in the name of the Lord Jesus, giving. (Colossians 3:17 NKJV)

FULL CIRCLE

Full circle: "A development has or will occur, leading a result or outcome back to the original source or situation."[9]

It's a familiar adage. I find that in life, full circles do not appear randomly or quickly. It often takes time and inspiration to make the connections, to witness the inherent need we all have to fill in the blanks of why and where. Still, I have been blessed to witness those moments.

I must be honest, sometimes there is second-guessing in volunteering. After committing, life gets in the way, tumbling over the best intentions to help. Questions make a genuine desire to help appear differently: Will I really make a difference here? Today, with other worries and projects, I am guilty of second-guessing. After all these years, I've learned to lean harder into the truth that the Holy Spirit has *guided* this encounter, and today inspired a friend to call me and ask for help.

Sunday morning finds me volunteering at the makeshift food bank. Our local community has grown as residents from nearby counties arrive, taking refuge from recent storms. They wait in

9 *OUP Dictionary* (Oxford University Press, 2015).

shelters for news of their community and a hoped-for return home. Resources are needed. The overwhelming line of people at the entrance of the food bank breaks my heart. Dear God, where do I begin?

The food bank is divided into two sections: relief supplies and immediate community supplies. Volunteers stack crates of water, nonperishables, and toiletries on trucks to transport them to smaller, devastated towns. The reality of human need hits hard as I see boxes of baby food, diapers, and blankets.

My friend Tom walks me to the immediate community supplies table. On this side of the building, people receive food and supplies to take home now. Volunteers are handed a checklist completed by those in line. Every volunteer is partnered with another to fill the box efficiently. For hours, I repeat the same routine: collect items, pack the box, and then return the box to the delivery table for perishable items to be added.

As I place another box on the table, I collect the checklist on my corner and hear a small voice call out, "Hello." A little girl stands, holding her mother's hand. They are next in line. She is so young. I stop, say hello, and introduce myself. I notice the little girl is holding a rag doll with black yarn hair in two braids tied with purple and yellow yarn. She's curious. "People here need food too? Can I help? Can I pick out something to send them? Can I help by sending that?" She points to one of the packages of water that has been set aside for her and her mother. Her mother nods. Tom quickly hands the little girl a black marker and asks if she would like to write something on the package for the person who will receive it. She writes a note. Then she places her doll on the table, carefully unties the braids, collects the purple and yellow yarn, and looks at us. Immediately, we all help as her little fingers reach through edges, tying a purple and yellow bow on two bottles. I peek at her note: "Jesus Love Us All." A selfless child, giving something precious in actions and words to comfort others. As we work to prepare her box, I hear Tom share how happy the package will make someone. He says this as he seamlessly packs replacement water bottles in her food box. I wonder if Tom is thinking about his little girls at home, safe with their mom. I think I can volunteer a bit longer.

A week later, a humble breakfast gathering is offered to express appreciation for all volunteers. As we eat, a story by a volunteer named Ben catches my attention. When Ben delivered relief supplies to a medical shelter, he heard about a woman who was left stranded on a roof during the storms, holding her one-year-old son for six hours. The woman and her son reached a shelter where Ben was volunteering. Ben saw her sitting on a cot, holding her son. Next to her were two empty water bottles and a wet Bible. Ben brought her some food, a package of bottled water, and blankets. He talked with her, listening to her ordeal. Suddenly, the woman began to weep and pointed at the writing on the package of bottled water: "Jesus Loves Us All."

"She handed me the wet Bible, creased open on Romans 8:26. Does anyone know the verse?" asks Ben, his voice shaking a bit as he looks away, taking in the scene again as it is his to share. "Inside the package of bottled water were two individual bottles with ribbons tied around them! Like a special delivery! She had gotten a special delivery, something personalized just for her! It was water for the body and food for the soul. It was unbelievable."

Silence takes over. I glance at Tom, several seats away. He is thinking the same thing I am: full circle. Tom's voice breaks as the two halves come together to create a complete story, full circle. Tangible evidence that we are still relevant in the universe, evidence that we are still led to help others in ways we cannot imagine will become lifetime outcomes.

"I know that verse," he says. "I can paraphrase it, mostly. 'In the same way the Spirit also helps our weakness; for we do not know how to pray as we should, but the Spirit Himself intercedes for us with groanings too deep for words … He intercedes … according to the Will of God.' Some of us know the beginning of that story, Ben."

I glance at Ben as he hears our parts in the story. He quickly wipes away the tears in his eyes as he thanks us for sharing and then thanks us again. Yet I can no longer see Ben as my tears blur my vision. What are the odds? Full circle.

No one has seen God at any time. If we love one another, God abides in us, and His love has been perfected in us. (1 John 4:12 NKJV)

FORECAST: HEAVY RAIN

One of the most difficult aspects of moving to a new place and setting up a home is finding those locations that will feel like and be a spiritual and emotional haven for you. What community projects will I volunteer in? Who needs my help? Where will my spiritual gifts be of service? Where is my new church? What will my new religious and spiritual family be like? Of all the necessary questions for adjustment, there are two constants that I can always rely on: leading and unknown weather forecasts.

God always leads and makes the necessary introductions happen for me to serve where He needs me. There are places where I volunteer my time, and family and friends honestly say, "I would have never seen you participating in that project!" That is part of saying, "Send me": You never know where God needs ambassadors.

The second constant I know for sure is that God's introductions do not come with an inclement weather warning. Whether it is physical or emotional, I cannot predict if my location of service will experience sunshine, clouds, rain, or heavy storms. The best I can do is to prepare by constantly praying that I will have the necessary heavenly gear to get me through whatever comes. In that preparation, I am not alone.

Gracious women and men have prayed, "Send me," but it always begins with a recalled admission: "Here am I." It's not that God needs to know where our geographical location is in order to put us to work.

Rather, it is a willingness to admit we are ready for service regardless of weather. That's not an easy task. Think about it: Ready for service *regardless* of weather. Imagine for a moment all the pictures and images you have seen of what's left after a hurricane, tornado, or heavy storm. Are you still willing to serve?

Would you rescind your offer to serve because the sun is too hot or the air is too humid? Would you rescind your offer to serve because you know where you may end up is not a friendly place or is dangerous in any way? God willing, we simply serve and rely on Him to help us through any weather. The forecast uncertain, we may be fortunate enough to get a warning of any impending storm. What do we do with the possibility of a dangerous weather forecast? When we hear it coming, how do we prepare for a storm?

It was a day of good news for me. A regular physical checkup indicated I was in good health. Actually, my physician said, "Everything still looks perfect. You are a miracle and a blessing. Go and continue enjoying life!" For anyone who has known my personal story, I can only attribute "miracle and blessing" to God, not science. Continued good health? That is a blessing I never take for granted. Yes, it was a day of good news! Yet in my sunshine, I heard the sound of thunder and heavy rain.

That evening, as I served in a new volunteer community, I found myself going through a familiar routine of donning a mask, gloves, and gown before entering a room to visit a patient. It was a pleasant visit. A man of faith, he shared a brief synopsis of his life and thanked me for my visit. He suffered no delusion that his body would recover from illness and was at peace. As with many people in the same community, he had outlived family and friends. He was on his own, but he was quick to say, "I am not alone—no matter what it looks like."

As I concluded my visit, he asked me to pray. I held his hand, and once my prayer was completed, I felt a gentle squeeze of my hand as he began to pray. It is not often that this happens, and I was humbled to hear his voice lift up words of gratitude and praise to God for all the kindness and joy of the day. The tone of his voice was strong and determined, but his words demonstrated Jesus was not only his Savior but also his friend. The honest words made tears pool in my eyes. And then I heard my new friend share a weather forecast: "God, keep this young woman on this righteous path. Help her stay the course. And when the storm comes, give her strength to run ahead of chariots, creating a path through heavy rain where You lead. Send your angels to sustain her."

Hours later, in the safety and comfort of my home, I read the story of Elijah and Ahab. It is a familiar story. In my mind's eye, I can imagine the scene. As a child, growing up in the Caribbean, I remember the sight of rain so thick you could not see but inches ahead. How thick was that heavy rain for Elijah? Is it possible to imagine that same heavy rain as being not just physical but emotional? How many times have I asked God for guidance through a storm? How many times has He sent someone to help me through a storm?

My good news day ended with prayers of gratitude, prayers of comfort for my new friend, and prayers for purpose: "Here I am. As you have blessed me for so long and kept me for so long, send me. Even if it storms." Throughout the hours of the night, the sound of thunder grew, and the winds changed.

Twenty hours later, a new morning, a new reality. A pandemic.

The early hours of the day find me sitting in my car, dialing a familiar phone number: my parents. I am calling to ask for continued prayers. I am headed to work through a heavy storm, and I am not the only one. As I begin the journey forward, I remember the prayer of my friend: "Help her stay the course." My good news day is now a reminder of how much I must rely on God to run through all of life's storms. To be in the trenches means to serve in faith, truly moving through the unseen and unpredictable. To be in trenches means to accept some level of risk. But as my friend reminded me, "I am not alone—no matter what it looks like."

The request, so obvious to me now, that all of us stay the course, that we run forward together with the purpose of ministry and mission, true light bearers in the deep dark. The one still voice can be used to bring calm and bring peace amid the noise. In every capacity, we are prepared, secured, and comforted with God's promises. Promises so clear we should not fear stumbling in our capacity to share the peace they bring: Here we are. Send us!

As I stand in line to be screened for temperature checks and answer questions, I watch the intake nurse holding a clipboard and thermometer. I notice her hands are shaking, and she nervously hands out masks and points to hand sanitizers as she begins checking boxes with information. I know her. We have worked in the emergency room trauma bay during regular shifts. She is a kind nurse. She recognizes me and waves me over to a different line with clinical staff intake. As she is writing down the temperature notes and filling in the boxes of questions regarding potential exposure, a silence fills the space between us. I decide to share with her that just a few days ago, a friend prayed for me and specifically asked that I stay the course through any storm. The nurse stops writing and looks at me. Quietly she asks, "Will we be able to stay the course, chaplain? How bad is the weather expected to be?"

"Heavy rain," I say and give her a reassuring nod. She looks down and nods for a minute.

"Are we ready?" she asks as she jots down final notes.

Yes, we are.

I will say of the Lord, "He is my refuge and my fortress; My God, in Him I will trust."(Psalm 91:2 NKJV)

Epilogue: Cartography of Faith

"Some things you learn best in calm and some in storm."[10]

I have known both.

I drop the last journal into a packing box. That's ten boxes of journals. Ten boxes detailing a journey I never expected. This is the only tangible proof of who I was and what I have gone through. These will be the only boxes I pack. The contents are too personal and precious to trust to anyone who fails to understand their content. I look around at the chaos surrounding me.

It is late in the evening. In my apartment in Orem, Utah, my parents are helping me pack. My life is represented in boxes—small boxes, big boxes, boxes full of clothes, books, and memories. I can hear the distinct sound of tape being pulled off the dispenser and rolling over the seams of boxes. Closure. Temporary or permanent? Who knows which boxes I will open first? Or never.

In fourteen hours, we will travel down an unknown road. Earlier, Dad plotted a path on an atlas. He opened the oversized book, looked at the options, and then closed the book. He pushed it aside and said he had found our way there, no worries. But exhaustion and doubt roam about the apartment, and I find his words to be of little comfort.

---

[10] Willa Cather, *The Song of the Lark*, 1915.

I have little to offer this expedition, even though this journey is for me. Mom and Dad have taken time away from work to spend the holiday moving me to a different state, a state of being and a state of location. A new beginning somewhere. Anywhere but here.

Collecting mail at my apartment mailbox has become an athletic feat. As I walk through heavily packed snow to pick up mail, I stop to look at the mountains. Beautiful. Utah, a place I have called home for years. How long? Who knows? The calendar I look at each day is one outlining teaching schedules and oncology treatments. A calendar that tells me when and where to show up but provides no promises of what will happen when I arrive. As I wade through piles of snow and clumsy motions between mittens and a tiny mailbox key, I find only one letter in my mailbox. My heart drops into the snow as I see the letter is from Texas Woman's University. Am I in?

I sit in my favorite spot in the world: the lake. It is a short drive from my home. There are benches and a view that truly no skilled painter could capture. I am meeting my friend Viola here. Four weeks ago, Viola's daughter, Julia, died two days before the end of her chemotherapy infusion trials. Two days. She had endured so much treatment for three years! Julia was my best friend. As I see Viola's car pull into the parking lot, I notice the car seat. All that is left as evidence of Julia's life is her precious five-year-old son. What will be the evidence of my life?

We sit and talk for a while. I tell Viola that on my last night of semester teaching, my college students brought a cake and balloons. They prepared a banner that said, "Good Luck!" and we simply spent time with one another. The celebration ended with words of goodwill, hugs, and a gift: a disposable camera to take pictures of my trip. Viola smiles as she listens. She has cared for me so many times through this journey of uncertainty. She has been family to me. Julia was family to me.

I show her the letter from the university. She reads it, carefully holding it by the edges with her gloves. Then she looks at me and says, "It's time. God has kept you alive through a trial in which you alone survived. There is no one left but you. This is not a coincidence or a mistake. This is God's work at hand." Holding the letter, she closes her eyes and whispers, "Praise God, this is a new start, child. A new beginning for you. Embrace it, and journey with God." Her smile and tears are truly genuine, and I know they come from a place of prayer and faith. "This, my child, is your next journey. It will be a blessed journey. Move forward, but don't forget where you've been. I will look out for your book. The story of what we have been through. Nurture that spiritual gift of writing."

I hold up the camera and take a place of where we are sitting, the beautiful view, because I don't want to forget where I have been.

The room is colder than usual. I sit in the chair, not far from the examination table. I am not sitting up there today. Today I get to wear my regular clothes, not the hospital gown, and I get to speak to my doctor on a level plane.

There is nothing unfamiliar about this room. I can tell you how many tiles there are on the floor and the contents of each cabinet and drawer. This has been more than an oncology consultation room for years. I usually sit on the examination table in a small frock, freezing, waiting for the oncologist, phlebotomist, nurse, or radiologist. Sometimes it seems like it's just for a moment, but sometimes I can feel the waiting seep into my day, stealing precious hours from me, more so than the cancer itself. All I do is wait.

I have been part of a trial and then case study for years. Today I get news about my treatment. The doctors tell me I am a medical mystery and that I, "must have the most amazing faith to get through this." Some days, that almost sounds believable. If I think about how I have affected future oncology treatment, the progress, and how others may not have to endure what I did, maybe this could all make sense. Maybe. Otherwise, I have simply lost all my friends in this oncology ward. I was the first one expected to die. With such an aggressive cancer, I was the first one expected to die. Yet here I am, the last one standing where hopeful souls once stood with me.

I hear the familiar voice of my physician outside the closed door. And there she is, walking through, healthy and vibrant, with a piece of paper that determines my future. She sits next to me, her familiar blue eyes lively. There is a smile on her face. "Good news," she says. And I wait.

It is always more difficult for others. Acceptance of a loved one's terminal diagnosis is a terminal diagnosis for those who love us as well. I have seen it, and I feel it to be true. I know what my mind and body are capable of, but my family will only see my journey through this. This will break them. It will emotionally rip them apart! This cannot be good. I am scared. The thought of anything else has simply left my mind. What is the worst-case scenario? I need to know.

The journey is quick: Visit to a physician, visit to an oncologist, diagnosis, bleak outcome of four months. I never knew I was that ill. Married for less than a year, I had not counted that one marriage vow to be the first one to tackle: Till death do us part. As I sit in the third physician visit, I am aware that the appointments for the day have been scheduled one immediately after the other; no minute has been wasted.

"The bottom line is that you have a very aggressive cancer, and you are very young," says the oncologist. "There are only two clinical trials you can participate in. Being in a trial does not mean you will survive or even go into remission. You will have to sign many documents, nondisclosure documents, and all you go through will most likely be for the benefit of others, so others may live. Do you understand that?" My ears are ringing as if I have been within dangerous perimeters of a bomb exploding. Remnants of my life (job, family, friends, graduate school) blown to pieces in seconds. Why would I not understand that? Finally, all the visits have yielded the proverbial bottom line. This is it. This is what is in front of me to deal with. The physician sits next to me and gives me information packets. Only two trials are available. Where?

"The first one is right here in Maryland," she says. "You can go to the location today. The second one is quite far away, in Utah. I will be honest; they have a remarkable team there, and the facility was built for this trial."

I hold my breath. What is this feeling that just entered the room? It's like a silent reminder has entered the room, but I don't know what is inside the void. Just a few months ago, my spouse accepted a job in Utah. How is that possible? I sit in silence as I weigh the options in my head. I can stay here and put my family through enormous pain as I endure treatment and potentially die as a casualty of a medical trial. Or I can go to Utah, where I am far from everyone, and nobody will know what I am going through. No worries for anyone! The physician hears my loud silence and understands it to be a shock.

"I don't know that you have the luxury of time," she says. "I know they will give you a thorough workup before you are accepted, but based on what I see …"

"Utah," I say. "Tell me how we begin. We, my husband, we, are moving to Utah. He has a job there and …" That's all that I can say. I don't tell her there is a slim possibility it will truly be a "we"; I am in this alone. But I choose to simply push that reality to the back of the room, stand at the door, and just hope … hope. What am I hoping for again?

"You were already going to move to Utah?" The physician looks at me with exaggerated surprise and shock, a look I will see over and over again in the next few days and for the rest of this journey. "You must have great favor in heaven! It's as if this was meant to be!" And just like that, her words remind me of what has entered the room and what I have forgotten: faith. Did it come for me? Or did someone send it? I have but a sliver of faith right now. During all these meetings and the final diagnosis, I have not invited faith or God into this space of despair and shock. I have assumed God is present, yet I am unfamiliar with these spaces, and they are truly dark and hopeless! For the second time that day, I push *that* reality to the back of the room and stand at the door, alone. Less than a week later, I arrive in Utah. I choose to carry the weight of silence. It is a heavy burden. I have no idea how my life will manage to continue a seemingly organized path. I cannot even see the path yet.

I close the door to an empty apartment. The morning is gray and cold. Fall has long passed, and winter has gripped the mountains. My future has been plotted as carefully as our route: Straight ahead, no left, no right. It is time to head to a new place, a new home. As I unlock the car, I see the disposable camera. Maybe one last picture of the mountains; I will miss them. Carelessly, I turn around and snap the photo, not taking time to even frame the photo or look back to see with my own eyes what the lens could warn us about.

Two hours later, we drive in silence. The road is impenetrable. Mom travels in the vehicle with me. The only guidance I have is the taillights of the U-Haul my dad is driving in front of me. We are traveling at less than ten miles per hour. Angry winds blow snow all around us. Our first hours of driving have placed us in the middle of a storm so severe I cannot imagine how there is any visibility ahead. My spirits are low, and the only grounding I feel is the traction of my vehicle rolling over the tire marks left by the truck ahead. I am simply following, wondering if this was a good idea or not.

I lie sleepless. My parents are asleep in the adjoining room. Christmas found us stranded somewhere between Utah and Colorado. There was no special holiday gathering or meal. Just us. Earlier, we sat at a table at a fast-food restaurant and watched the snow keep falling, building. The town we are in has been shut down by the perilous weather. Only one hotel and one fast-food place are open in this town, and we are fortunate to be in them. Watching the snowfall, it feels as if I am sitting inside a snow globe a child had violently shaken, and there is no hope of clarity amid the constantly shifting environment.

How did we get here? My eyes fall on the atlas that has made its way to my backpack. As I leaf through it, I see the clusters of multicolored lines, the empty spaces that run off the page. Maps—a guide, a visual guide to observing the populated and newly discovered terrains of the world. I don't believe maps have ever lacked humanity. What are the markers we recognize, the ones outside the span of a map or the pages of an atlas? Those markers that let us know we are almost there, like a gravel road, a magnificent tree, or the last hill on the journey home. Maps are a guide to keep the explorer, the traveler, or the one embarking on a journey safe. It shouldn't be expected that said journey would be perilous. But if you don't know where you are going, is it not dangerous to move forward? Maybe maps were intended to entirely avoid the perilous parts of the journey. How long have we relied on cartography to help us traverse spaces?

Of interest to me are not the lines that delineate how to get from Point A to Point B. Of greater value to me is the question of space. The area outside those lines, the space between. Our journey, *this* journey, transcended the lines of a map. Some journeys begin with the best of intentions. Some, like ours, are full of great hope and faith, the emotions that linger on the margins of any map. I trace my finger along the line, the "road" to Texas. New Year's will still find us traveling on this road.

The phone call was brief. My father, traveling for work, has called to say hello. It's time. He can hear it in my voice. This is not how I wanted to share the news. I have survived something they were unaware of, and I will continue in treatment, but not here. I thought he would be proud that I was able to work as a professor at the university through this adversity and that I completed my master's program. But that information is irrelevant. He is taking a detour to come and visit me.

Many hours later, I stand at the terminal in the airport, waiting for my father. I see him. I forgot what joy has eluded me by consistently telling my family I was too busy to travel home for the holidays or working on research for my master's. I have missed my family! But I was not ready for them to see me. I was not ready for them to know. No excuses now.

I see my father walking through the terminal. I see my father walk right past me. Did he not hear me? As I turn around to follow him, I catch a glimpse of my reflection in the glass windows lining the terminal's passageway. *He didn't recognize me!* Suddenly, all that has been taken and stripped out of me seems tangible. I am not who I used to be. Surviving was a temporal, pyrrhic victory. I call out to him one time and then twice. He turns, looks around, and then sees me. Speechless. The steps between us automatically fill him in on what has been my life for years. If I had three wishes, I would ask for this moment to be dissolved.

The road is dangerous. I should know this. What was meant to be a two-day journey has become a long traverse. On our seventh day of travel, the snow has not stopped, but the temperature is rising. With one lane to travel in, the snow around us sometimes reaches the height of my vehicle's window. At any point where the snow has become ice, trucks venture over it to pass the slow traffic. The road is dangerous.

As we begin a downhill crawl, I notice the truck behind me is taking the left lane and passing us. As one truck begins to pass us, I notice another truck behind me traveling at a faster speed. The truck on my left splashes snow, mud, and sand on my windshield. My quick attempts to clean the windshield prove useless as a light on my dashboard begins to blink: There is no windshield wiper fluid. After days of silent travel, I finally hear my voice claim my human condition: "Help me! I can't see where I am going!"

As soon as the words leave me, I feel a blast of cold air as my mother lowers the passenger window and looks ahead, directing my driving, leading me forward. I barely hear her above the incessant screaming of the truck's horn. After half a mile of driving blind, an exit has appeared. I pull into the first gas station we encounter. As I turn off the engine, my entire body is shaking. Now I truly appreciate the danger, uncertainty, and the perilous journey we are on. I recognize it as if I have been oblivious to it all along.

I am the only customer in the small convenience store. A sign on the door reads, "Cash Only. Storm." I find the last two blue bottles of windshield wiper fluid. My hands are still shaking as I hand the money to the old man, a stranger behind the cash register. He tells me he hasn't seen snow like this in over ten years. He tells me none of the machines work because electricity is out in many places. He tells me the roads should not be traveled in this weather. Then he asks, "Where are you headed?" I tell him Denton, Texas.

The stranger closes the registrar drawer and offers to carry the heavy bottles to my car. He helps me refill the empty fluid tank, he cleans the windshield for me, and meets my mother. He tells me to wait a minute. *Wait?* I watch him walk to a pick-up and bring out two more blue bottles. He places them in the trunk of my car. "You can't be too sure about those roads," he says. "Best take the extra bottles. No charge." He shakes my hand and tells me to drive safely. Then he walks back into the store. I never thanked him.

We begin our travel before the sun comes up. I am driving alone. We have weathered the storm and will reach Texas today. What will happen? The journey on the dark road is slow. Then suddenly, something beautiful happens. The sun comes out. The beauty of the colors is amazing. As I follow my parents into a small location for breakfast, I fumble to find the disposable camera, the gift from my students. I must take a picture of this! I have never seen anything like it!

We travel a few hours more. Unexpectedly, I see my father pull into a gas station. We don't need a break. What could be happening?

He tells me it's time to call the university. I pull out the business card for Dr. Burns, the department chair for the Rhetoric program. It's January 2. Nobody will be in the office. My father does not listen to my arguments but simply hands me a phone.

One ring, two rings. Dr. Burns is there. His cheerful voice is a welcome sound. "Ms. Rodriguez! We have been expecting you! Classes begin on Monday. Let me give you some enrollment codes. I trust you have had a wonderful journey?" As I write the enrollment codes down, my father takes out a credit card from his wallet. As Dr. Burns transfers me to the registrar's office, my father says, "Pay for the classes. Make sure you are enrolled, and then we will keep driving." I hold back tears as I talk to the registrar. Is this really happening?

"What is the title of your book? I know you must have it already," says Viola as we sit on the bench. I do have a title, but it is truly a working title.

"The Waiting Room," I say. "It's a play on the word and space." Viola looks and smiles at me. She tells me it's a perfect title. She encourages me to share the stories of *our* medical trials. Not the medical part but the parts that settled in the waiting room. Nobody will understand. Nobody would believe it.

"You will send me the second copy? The first one is for your mother to have and be proud," says Viola. She knows my apprehension is heavier than my desire. "This is not the first time you will have stories to share. You will go forward and gather more stories, different stories. Put breadth and depth into this experience. We are so blessed. My daughter was so blessed. Watching all of you … You will know when the time is right for these stories."

I don't tell her the stories are already written, journaled every day. I don't tell her that the journals get tossed into a box in the corner of my closet. I don't tell her that every journal is distinct in the amount of pain it delivers through memories. I am not ready. I will collect more stories before I share *those* stories. To this day, long after Viola has passed and long after Julia's son has graduated from law school, "The Waiting Room" remains a dusty manuscript in a weathered binder. The only person who read the manuscript was my mother. She left tear stains on the pages and sat in my home, looking out the window and thanking God for His mercy. Everything I had kept to myself for years was shared in black and white, and reading it served as a familiar echo of events. Sharing those stories with my mother interrupted that echo in my soul. A penny dropped in a tin can, that's the sound of an interrupted echo. What felt heavy sounds quite empty. I shared a journey only when I got to the other side. I didn't know it would create such surprise, hurt, and gratitude for God's grace. Years later, when my mom died quite unexpectedly, I retrieved the manuscript I had left in her safekeeping, wrapped it in a quilt, and stuffed it in a box in the back of a different closet. The pen felt too heavy, and I put it down. I waited. I wait.

We sit in a small office across the desk from Amber. Right now, she has all the power and authority in the room. Amber is the apartment manager, and she explains why there is no vacancy. "Classes begin this coming Monday. There was a waiting list. We are full. You should have called months ago to ensure one of our units was available."

A waiting list. Even in a new environment, I am destined to wait. My father sits calmly with his coat on and his hat in his hands. He looks at Amber and, in a kind, respectful voice, says, "Would you check again? You see, we have traveled a long way to get here." He pauses, leans into the desk, and with a determined smile says, "*This* is where we are meant to be."

I look at my family. They are tired. I have traveled to Texas on borrowed strength. They carried me along the dangerous path because I was not able to walk it on my own. Their faith is unbreakable. I was raised to understand the strength of faith, the necessity of prayer, the companionship of traveling with God. They are the shoulders

I stand on right now. God, the Author of this journey, has opened many doors. Still, we wait.

As Amber checks her computer, a knock on the door distracts her. The gentleman at the door wears a maintenance uniform. He apologizes for the interruption and updates her on the maintenance crew's work on apartment 401. "The paint is dry, and we just installed the carpet. It's ready to go," he says and leaves as quickly as he appeared.

I watch as Amber slowly withdraws her hands from the computer keyboard, and with wide eyes, looks at my father, who nods in greater understanding of the events. "*That* is *our* apartment," he says with a smile, and Amber draws up the rental contract.

I awake alarmed, as if someone has just recklessly disregarded my need for rest. I immediately find my surroundings foreign. The small apartment seems too big. This is where I will begin a new life. This is where the lines on the map are still to be drawn. Feelings I haven't revisited during the journey have traveled miles to find me, and they have arrived. I am alone here.

I get up and walk to the window. I pull aside the blinds, hoping the U-Haul is still there, that my parents are still here. No U-Haul. No snow. The day is clear. It feels like spring. I see my itinerary of classes carefully written out on a piece of paper next to my computer. I need to pick up textbooks for tomorrow, my first day of doctoral studies.

As I pull into the university bookstore parking lot, I am intimidated. Everyone knows where they are going. On the bookstore door is a sign: "Please Leave Backpacks with Attendant." As I place my backpack on the counter, my hand feels the front pocket. What is that? The disposable camera? Where in the world does anyone have film developed these days?

Five hours later, I stand by the counter of a local pharmacy where my disposable camera film has been developed. The photo attendant watches me open the envelope and carefully remove the three pictures that were on the roll. "Are you OK?" he asks. "Do you need to sit down? You look kinda pale. Are you feeling dizzy?"

I carefully place all three photographs on the counter in order of succession. "Some things you learn best in the calm," I look at the picture of the lake where Viola and I sat, "and some in the storm." I look at the picture of the angry blizzard coming over the mountains minutes before our departure from Utah. Would we have ventured on this journey if we had seen this storm chasing us, taking us over, grounding us? The storm that lengthened our journey by days. The storm that we went through by faith, with continuous prayers, with my doubts of the outcomes. And there it is, the last photograph of the unexpected. The beautiful sunrise provided by the great cartographer of our journey. A promise that the storm had passed. A sacred respite. A sacred awareness. This is the evidence of my life, now. Three images capture years and experiences I cannot begin to speak of. It is tangible evidence of a perilous journey with safe passage: a cartography of faith.

As Christians, we know the destination, and we must rely on God to lead us in the journeys. I pick up the pen with a different purpose now. Unaware of all that will come, of all the additional storms that will bend me again, I am blessed to be aware of the spaces between the lines in the cartography of life. The spaces filled with grace, mercy, and forgiveness. I volunteer, teach, and minister in these spaces. Often these are found on the margins of the atlas, unmarked but traveled into by faith. I am not the only one that traverses into the small lines on the map, sharing stories of how great and good God is. Sharing stories with a prayer and an honest attempt to encourage, inspire, and wonder. We all search the obvious with great care. In this season of my life, surrounded by transformative experiences, a cartography of faith delivers the sum of it all in a simple but tried-and-true statement: We are not irrelevant to God; He will always lead us, walk with us, and love and shelter us through storms.

"Seek the Lord and His strength,"[11] and be amazed and comforted in the shared stories of God's faithfulness.

Whoever dwells in the shelter of the Most High, will rest in the shadow of the Almighty. I will say of the Lord, "He is my refuge and my fortress, my God, in whom I trust ... He will cover you with his feathers, and under his wings you will find refuge. (Psalm 91:1-2, 4 NKJV)

[11] 1 Chronicles 16:11 (NIV).

About the Author

Chaplain, professor, public speaker, and award-published writer Dr. Dixil Lisbeth Rodriguez serves in various health-care, education, and humanitarian communities. She now divides her time between Texas and Ohio.

Printed in the United States
by Baker & Taylor Publisher Services